S0-ATB-997

HTML5 Media

HTML5 Media

Shelley Powers

O'REILLY®

Beijing · Cambridge · Farnham · Köln · Sebastopol · Tokyo

HTML5 Media
by Shelley Powers

Copyright © 2011 Shelley Powers. All rights reserved.
Printed in the United States of America.

Published by O'Reilly Media, Inc., 1005 Gravenstein Highway North, Sebastopol, CA 95472.

O'Reilly books may be purchased for educational, business, or sales promotional use. Online editions are also available for most titles (*http://my.safaribooksonline.com*). For more information, contact our corporate/institutional sales department: (800) 998-9938 or *corporate@oreilly.com*.

Editor: Simon St. Laurent
Production Editor: Kristen Borg
Proofreader: O'Reilly Production Services

Cover Designer: Karen Montgomery
Interior Designer: David Futato
Illustrator: Robert Romano

Nutshell Handbook, the Nutshell Handbook logo, and the O'Reilly logo are registered trademarks of O'Reilly Media, Inc. *HTML5 Media*, the image of a brown-eared pheasant, and related trade dress are trademarks of O'Reilly Media, Inc.

Many of the designations used by manufacturers and sellers to distinguish their products are claimed as trademarks. Where those designations appear in this book, and O'Reilly Media, Inc., was aware of a trademark claim, the designations have been printed in caps or initial caps.

While every precaution has been taken in the preparation of this book, the publisher and authors assume no responsibility for errors or omissions, or for damages resulting from the use of the information contained herein.

ISBN: 978-1-449-30445-4

[LSI]

1312548526

Table of Contents

Preface

Flash is dead.

At least, that's what we're told: thanks to the introduction of the HTML5 `video` and `audio` elements, Flash is now dead.

Of course, we know this statement isn't true: Flash will have its place in web pages for many years to come. However, thanks to the new HTML5 media elements, we're no longer totally dependent on Flash in order to embed a playable audio or video file in our web pages.

In years past, to play audio or video resources in a web page we had to use Flash (or some other plug-in) that may, or may not, work correctly with all browsers. Many times we'd have to use a combination of object elements, embeds, and links, just to ensure that a video could be played. It wasn't unusual to find the following in web pages:

```
<object width="425" height="350">
    <param name="movie" value="http://www.youtube.com/v/7_6B6vwE83U">
    </param>
    <embed src="http://www.youtube.com/v/7_6B6vwE83U"
    type="application/x-shockwave-flash" width="425" height="350">
    </embed>
</object>
```

Though we could get a video or audio resource to play, we couldn't really do anything with it. We certainly couldn't provide custom controls, ensure subtitle support, or use something like SVG or the `canvas` element with it.

Beginning with HTML5, though, we now have two elements—`audio` and `video`—that provide the long overdue functionality we've needed to really take advantage of audio and video in web pages. Best of all, solid support for the media element's basic functionality is already available in all modern browsers and in most mobile environments.

So while Flash isn't dead, it also isn't the only option we have, and having more options is a very good thing.

As I note in Chapter 1, Flash is still essential if you want your video or audio file to play in older browsers.

About this Book

This book is tightly focused on two new HTML5 elements: the audio and video elements.

In Chapter 1, I introduce both and discuss issues of embedding the elements in web pages, how to mark up the elements based on quality and type of audio and video file, as well as exploring all the options available by default with both elements.

In Chapter 2, I describe how to customize the appearance of the media elements using CSS, as well as how to create your own applications that control and work with the elements. I also provide an introduction into debugging your HTML5 media applications, as well as how to check out current browser support.

In Chapter 3, I discuss some of the upcoming media functionality, including support for multiple audio and video tracks, and the new media controller that synchronizes several different media elements. We'll also explore the track element, the caption and subtitle formats SRT and WebVTT, and how to enable support for both now using JavaScript libraries.

In Chapter 4, I explore some of the more advanced and esoteric uses of the media elements. This includes integrating the media elements with both SVG (Scalable Vector Graphics) and the canvas element to create the rather amazing effects you may have seen online. I'll also introduce you to upcoming and potential API support for both media elements, including generating audio as well as playing it.

Book Audience

You'll get the most out of this book if you are a web developer, author, or designer who wants to get up to speed on the HTML5 audio and video elements. No actual experience is necessary with either audio or video files, as there are numerous examples freely available on the web you can use for the examples, and I provide enough information to ensure you can work with those examples. However, you'll get the most out of the book if you have worked with CSS and JavaScript before.

Though Chapter 4 does get into the canvas element and SVG, you don't need prior experience with either of these technologies in order to work with the examples.

Examples

O'Reilly provides a downloadable file with examples from this book. To be able to use the examples with a minimum of editing, most examples use generic names for audio and video files. Thus, audio files are called *audiofile*, with whatever extension is appropriate, and video files are called *videofile* with the appropriate extension. You can just use whatever video and audio files you have, renamed to match the examples, or change the examples to match your files.

I don't include actual video and audio files in the example because doing so would increase the size of the download file enormously. If you need example audio and video files, you can find freely available versions of each on the Internet. One video file I used with many of the examples is the short animated film Big Buck Bunny. This animated movie is fast becoming the *de facto* HTML5 video primarily because the video is provided in different formats, and is freely usable via its generous Creative Commons license.

You can read more about, and access Big Buck Bunny and other Blender Foundation videos at *http://www.blender.org/features-gallery/blender-open-projects/*. Blender is an open source and freely available tool for 3D content generation.

 In fact, you can easily find many different tools and utilities for working with audio and video files that are either freely available, shareware, or available for a 30 day trial. I cover some of these in the Appendix.

Another source for media files is the Internet Archive. This site has sections for both audio and video files that are either Creative Commons licensed for broad usage, or are in the Public Domain and freely available. The Library of Congress is also another great source for both video and audio files.

 The Internet Archive Moving Picture archive can be found at *http://www .archive.org/details/movies*, and the Audio archive is at *http://www.ar chive.org/details/audio*. Audio and video files can be found at the Library of Congress in the Digital Collections site at *http://www.loc.gov/library/ libarch-digital.html*.

Target Browsers

Throughout the book, you'll find me referring to *target browsers*. Since the video and audio elements are very new, the target browsers for this book are those that support both elements. At a minimum, this means Internet Explorer 9+, Firefox 3.5+, Opera 10.5+, Chrome 6+, and Safari 3.1+. At the time this book was written, the latest full release of each browser could work with the majority of examples in the book.

Some of the examples use more cutting edge CSS and JavaScript, such as the CSS3 transitions and transforms, These examples required beta, and in some cases, alpha software, to test. The alpha/beta software I used for these examples are IE 10, Firefox 6 (and 7), Opera Next, the Webkit Nightly build, and the Chrome Canary build. All but IE 10 are available in multiple operating system versions.

I'll make a point to note when alpha and beta software was required to ensure an example worked, or if an example only works in some browsers.

The Polyglot Question: HTML or XHTML?

HTML5 supports two different serializations: HTML and XHTML. HTML5 documents are served with a `text/html` MIME type, while XHTML5 documents are served with an `application/xml` or `application/xhtml+xml` MIME type. The majority of web pages are served as HTML.

There are differences in syntax between the two. HTML allows uppercase element and attribute names, unquoted attribute values, and you don't have to use closing tags, or the empty-tag syntax with void elements such as the `img` element:

```
<img src="somesource.jpg" alt="some desc" />
```

In addition, HTML allows you to use *boolean* attributes without values, while XHTML requires an assignment:

```
<video src="somemovie.mp4" controls="controls"></video>
```

There are other differences, but these are the ones I wanted to highlight.

The example pages in this book work only with the HTML serialization, primarily because I do make use of boolean attributes without assignment. I really dislike having to assign a kludge value to a boolean attribute. However, I also use quotes with attributes, close tags, and never use uppercase letters for elements and attributes. If you want to serve the example pages I provide as XHTML, you'll need to modify the examples accordingly.

 The WHATWG organization provides a Wiki page on polyglot differences between HTML and XHTML serializations at *http://wiki.whatwg .org/wiki/HTML_vs._XHTML*. There's also a formal document on the same at the W3C at *http://dev.w3.org/html5/html-xhtml-author-guide/ html-xhtml-authoring-guide.html*.

Conventions Used in This Book

The following typographical conventions are used in this book:

Italic
> Indicates new terms, URLs, email addresses, filenames, and file extensions.

`Constant width`
> Used for program listings, as well as within paragraphs to refer to program elements such as variable or function names, databases, data types, environment variables, statements, and keywords.

`Constant width bold`
> Shows commands or other text that should be typed literally by the user.

`Constant width italic`
> Shows text that should be replaced with user-supplied values or by values determined by context.

 This icon signifies a tip, suggestion, or general note.

 This icon indicates a warning or caution.

Using Code Examples

This book is here to help you get your job done. In general, you may use the code in this book in your programs and documentation. You do not need to contact us for permission unless you're reproducing a significant portion of the code. For example, writing a program that uses several chunks of code from this book does not require permission. Selling or distributing a CD-ROM of examples from O'Reilly books does require permission. Answering a question by citing this book and quoting example code does not require permission. Incorporating a significant amount of example code from this book into your product's documentation does require permission.

We appreciate, but do not require, attribution. An attribution usually includes the title, author, publisher, and ISBN. For example: "*HTML5 Media* by Shelley Powers (O'Reilly). Copyright 2011 Shelley Powers, 978-1-449-30445-4."

If you feel your use of code examples falls outside fair use or the permission given above, feel free to contact us at *permissions@oreilly.com*.

Safari® Books Online

Safari Safari Books Online is an on-demand digital library that lets you easily search over 7,500 technology and creative reference books and videos to find the answers you need quickly.

With a subscription, you can read any page and watch any video from our library online. Read books on your cell phone and mobile devices. Access new titles before they are available for print, and get exclusive access to manuscripts in development and post feedback for the authors. Copy and paste code samples, organize your favorites, download chapters, bookmark key sections, create notes, print out pages, and benefit from tons of other time-saving features.

O'Reilly Media has uploaded this book to the Safari Books Online service. To have full digital access to this book and others on similar topics from O'Reilly and other publishers, sign up for free at *http://my.safaribooksonline.com*.

How to Contact Us

Please address comments and questions concerning this book to the publisher:

O'Reilly Media, Inc.
1005 Gravenstein Highway North
Sebastopol, CA 95472
800-998-9938 (in the United States or Canada)
707-829-0515 (international or local)
707-829-0104 (fax)

We have a web page for this book, where we list errata, examples, and any additional information. You can access this page at:

http://www.oreilly.com/catalog/9781449304454

To comment or ask technical questions about this book, send email to:

bookquestions@oreilly.com

For more information about our books, courses, conferences, and news, see our website at *http://www.oreilly.com*.

Find us on Facebook: *http://facebook.com/oreilly*

Follow us on Twitter: *http://twitter.com/oreillymedia*

Watch us on YouTube: *http://www.youtube.com/oreillymedia*

Acknowledgments

Thanks to my editor, Simon St. Laurent, for providing me this opportunity to write about the wonderful new HTML5 media elements.

Thanks also to the production team, and Chris Mills for doing an outstanding job as technical reviewer/editor. My appreciations also to Ben Henick for his readability review of the text.

CHAPTER 1

HTML5 Audio and Video Elements: By-Default

The media elements, as the HTML5 `audio` and `video` elements are generically termed, are a way of embedding playable media files directly into a web page without having to use Flash or a plug-in. The elements can be styled with CSS, integrated with SVG and Canvas, and controlled with JavaScript.

Browsers and other user agents that implement the HTML5 media elements also provide default controls and behavior for each. In this chapter, I cover how to add HTML5 video and audio elements to your web page, and explore some of the implementation differences among the browsers. I also cover the more widely supported media file *codecs* and *containers*, and browser support for each.

Support for the media elements is relatively broad, though not all features of the media elements are supported in all browsers. Table 1-1 provides a listing of popular browsers and mobile environments, and the version of each that provides at least a minimum of support for the media elements.

Table 1-1. Support for HTML5 audio and video, by popular browser and mobile OS

User Agent	Version
Internet Explorer	9+
Google Chrome	3+
Firefox	3.5+
Opera	10.5+
Opera Mini	11+
Safari	3.1+
iOS	3.0+
Android OS	2.0+

Adding a Media Element to a Web Page

The HTML5 media elements share a common syntax and subgroup of attributes. The only difference between the two elements is the content they manage, and a small group of additional attributes for the `video` element.

Minimal Element Syntax

The simplest syntax to add a media element to the web page is demonstrated in Example 1-1. In the HTML, an `audio` element is used to embed an audio file encoded as Ogg Vorbis into the web page. The URL for the audio file is given in the `audio` element's `src` attribute. The element's style and behavior will be the default defined in the HTML5 specification and implemented by the browser.

Example 1-1. HTML5 web page with embedded audio file using an audio element

```
<!DOCTYPE html>
<head>
   <title>Audio</title>
   <meta charset="utf-8" />
</head>
<body>
   <audio src="audiofile.ogg">
   </audio>
</body>
```

The page validates as proper HTML5, and Firefox, Chrome, and Opera all support the file type. When you load the page in these browsers, you don't get an error. However, when you look at the page, you won't see anything.

Compare Example 1-1 with the following:

```
<!DOCTYPE html>
<head>
    <title>Video</title>
    <meta charset="utf-8" />
</head>
<body>
    <video src="videofile.ogv">
    </video>
</body>
```

Unlike the audio element, the video element has a play area that should show as long as there's no error loading the video, and the video element isn't deliberately hidden. If you want to actually see the audio file in the page, you need to add the `controls` attribute. Since `controls` is a *boolean* attribute, all you need do is add the attribute word:

```
<audio src="meadow.ogg" controls>
</audio>
```

A *boolean* attribute is one where a value doesn't need to be assigned to the attribute: its very presence implies a true value, while the lack of the attribute implies a default false value. However, *boolean* attributes must be assigned a value if you're serving your page up as XHTML, or you'll get a page error. The standard approach for XHTML5 is to assign the attribute a value equal to the attribute name, contained within quotes and without any extraneous white space (`controls="controls"`).

Figure 1-1 shows the audio element in Firefox after the `controls` attribute has been added. The control is rather plain, but it does the job. You now know an audio file has been added to the page, and you can start and stop the audio file, change the volume, and watch its progress as it plays.

Figure 1-1. Audio element with default control in Firefox 4

Disabled Scripting and the Magically Appearing Controls UI

Both the video and audio elements support the `controls` attribute for adding a default control UI (user interface) for the media resource. If you don't want the default control UI, leave the attribute off. Note, however, that something interesting happens with the control UI when scripting is disabled: in at least one browser, the control UI is added to the media element, whether you want it or not.

Web developers wanting to provide custom controls remove the `controls` attribute so that the default control doesn't conflict with the custom control. The developer typically adds the `controls` attribute to the video or audio element, and then removes it using script as soon as the media element is loaded. This form of *progressive enhancement* ensures that if scripting is disabled, the user can still play the media resource.

However, sometimes people deliberately leave the `controls` attribute off the media element because they're using the media element as part of a web page presentation and want the media to play as soon as the page loads—regardless of whether scripting is enabled or not. They'll remove the `controls` attribute, and add `autoplay` and possibly the `loop` attribute (covered later in the chapter). If scripting is enabled, the default media control isn't added to the page—but if scripting is disabled in the user's browser, according to the HTML5 specification, the browser is then supposed to add the control, by default.

This is an unusual event without precedent in web development. It's comparable to the browser overriding CSS to display hidden or collapsed fields if scripting is disabled, regardless of what the developer or author wants.

Currently, Opera is the only browser that actually provides a visible control if scripting is disabled. The other browsers are technically in violation of the HTML5 specification, though I couldn't find bugs for any of the browsers asking for this behavior. There are, however, bugs filed against the HTML5 specification to remove this unusual fallback feature. Since we don't know if the bugs will result in a change to the specification or not, you'll want to test your use of the HTML media elements with scripting enabled and disabled, regardless of whether you use scripting in your page or not.

Another browser foible: if scripting is disabled, Firefox doesn't currently display a control UI (User Interface) even if you do provide the `controls` attribute. You'll need to use the right mouse button context menu to control the media. More on this in Chapter 2.

Support for Multiple Media File Types

Figure 1-1 showed Example 1-1 in Firefox, using the default control UI that Firefox provides. You're probably curious to see what the default styling is for the `audio` element control in another browsers, such as Internet Explorer 9.x. If you open the page in IE 9, though, all you'll get is a black box with a small red x signaling broken content.

The reason you received an indication of broken content is because the `audio` element only features one type of audio content—an audio file encoded as Ogg Vorbis. Microsoft does not support Ogg Vorbis in Internet Explorer.

You can play Ogg Vorbis files in IE 9 if you install supporting software. I'll cover this in more detail in the next section.

Testing the page with all our target browsers, we find that the audio file works with Chrome, Opera, and Firefox, but not with Internet Explorer or Safari. In IE, the element appears broken, while in Safari the control appears but nothing happens when you hit the play button.

We'll get into the various audio and video codecs and browser support in the next section, but for now, let's see what we can do to ensure media files work with all of our target browsers. This time, though, we'll add a video element to the page.

In Example 1-2, the web page contains a video element, but rather than provide the location of the video file in the element's src attribute, three different video files are defined in three different source child elements. The location for each of the video files is given in the source element's src attribute.

Example 1-2. HTML5 web page with embedded video element with three separate video types

```
<!DOCTYPE html>
<head>
    <title>Video</title>
    <meta charset="utf-8" />
</head>
<body>
    <video id="meadow" controls>
        <source src="videofile.mp4" />
        <source src="videofile.ogv" />
        <source src="videofile.webm" />
    </video>
</body>
```

Both the video and audio elements can contain zero or more source elements. These child elements define a way to specify more than one audio or video file in different formats. If a browser doesn't support one format, hopefully it will find a format it supports in another source element.

 If you use the src attribute on the audio or video element, any contained source elements are ignored. Using both also generates a HTML5 validator conformance error. Use one or the other, but not both.

What happens if the browser or user agent does not find a video or audio file it supports? Both of the media elements do allow other HTML within their opening and closing tags, so can this other HTML be used as *fallback* content?

Unfortunately, the answer is "no". You can include other content in the media elements, but that content is only for browsers and other user agents that don't support either the audio or video elements. For instance, if you open a web page containing the HTML shown in Example 1-3 in an older browser, such as IE 8 (or IE 9 running in Compatibility View), the YouTube video is shown rather than the embedded video.

Example 1-3. HTML5 web page with embedded video element with three separate video types and fallback content for user agents that don't support HTML5 video

```
<!DOCTYPE html>
<head>
   <title>Big Buck Bunny Movie</title>
   <meta charset="utf-8" />
</head>
<body>
   <video controls>
      <source src="videofile.mp4" />
      <source src="videofile.ogv"  />
      <source src="videofile.webm" />
      <iframe width="640" height="390"
         src="http://www.youtube.com/embed/YE7VzlLtp-4">
      </iframe>
   </video>
</body>
```

Older browsers, such as IE 7 and IE 8, get the YouTube video, which ensures that web page readers using these older browsers have access to the material. However, if you remove the Ogg Vorbis and WebM source elements and open the page in Firefox, all you'll get is a square gray box with a lighter gray X because Firefox can't find a video source it can play. You *won't* get the YouTube video.

The only way to ensure that a video plays in all of the target browsers and other user agents is to provide all the appropriate video types.

 Before getting into the codecs, it's important to know that you can use video files with an audio element, and audio files with a video element. The only difference between the two is the video element provides a playing area. All browsers support video files with the audio element, but only Opera and Firefox currently support audio files playing in the video element. I strongly recommend using the appropriate element.

The Audio and Video File Babble and the Source Element in Detail

When talking about media file types, we're really talking about two separate components: the software used to encode and decode the audio or video stream (the *codec*, which is short for *compressor-decompressor* or *coder-decoder*), and the *container*, which is a wrapper format that contains the media streams and information about how the data and metadata co-exist. An example of a container is the open source Ogg (from Xiph.Org), while an example of a codec is VP8, a *lossy* video compression format from On2 (and Google). Technically, a codec could be used with many different containers, and containers could wrap many different codecs, but we tend to think of pairs of container/codecs when talking about browser support.

Audio files are containers wrapping one type of media data, the audio stream, but video files typically wrap two different media streams: the video and the audio data streams. In addition, containers can also support subtitles and captions, as well as the information to keep all data *tracks* in sync.

 Though you can embed subtitles directly into the file with some containers, HTML5 video provides a means of incorporating external subtitle files. More on incorporating subtitles and other accessible features in Chapter 3.

HTML5 Audio Codecs/Containers and Lossless versus Lossy Compression

Just like with image containers, such as JPEG and PNG, audio and video codecs can either be *lossless* or *lossy*. A lossless video or audio codec preserves all of the original media file's data when it's compressed. Lossy compression techniques, however, lose data each time the data is encoded.

Though most of us have the bandwidth to download lossless images such as PNGs, lossless video is beyond even the most generous of broadband capacity, so the only codecs supported for HTML5 video are lossy codecs. Audio, however, is different. The audio element supports uncompressed audio files, as well as audio files with both lossless and lossy codecs.

WAV Audio Format

One of the older and more familiar audio file formats is the Waveform Audio File Format (WAVE), commonly known as WAV for the extension the audio files are given (*.wav*). Though WAV files can support compression, most WAV files contain audio in an uncompressed Pulse-Code Modulation (PCM) representation, which means the files tend to be quite large.

Safari, Chrome, Firefox, and Opera support uncompressed WAV files. However, the size of the WAV files preclude their being a popular HTML5 audio file format.

MP3

Another well known and common audio file format is the MPEG-1 Audio Layer 3, commonly known as MP3 because of the extension given MP3 files (.mp3). It is neither a container or codec, as we know these things. Instead, it's an all-in-one lossy compressed audio file with metadata strategically inserted.

At this time, the only audio format that Microsoft supports in IE9 and up, by default, is MP3. In addition, the format is also supported by Safari and Chrome. However, Firefox and Opera refused to support MP3s right from the start, because of patent issues and royalty requirements.

MP3 is supported in most operating system environments, and MP3 files are a popular fallback when linked into the page. Though the file won't play natively in the browser, clicking the link will trigger some media player in most environments:

```
<audio id="background" autoplay loop>
   <source src="audiofile.mp3" type="audio/mpeg" />
   <source src="audiofile.ogg" type="audio/ogg" />
   <p><a href="audiofile.mp3">Your audio file fallback</a></p>
</audio>
```

Safari requires the installation of QuickTime and supports whatever media types QuickTime natively supports in the system. Since Quick-Time supports MP3 and WAV, Safari supports MP3 and WAV.

Ogg Vorbis

When the media elements were first added to HTML5, the specification included a requirement that all user agents support the Ogg open source container. The Ogg container was developed by the Xiph.Org foundation, which also developed an associated audio codec, called Vorbis. The Vorbis codec is a lossy compression technique that is free for everyone to use and is, according to the folks at Xiph.Org, free of patents (to the best of their determination). The hope at the time the media elements were first defined was that this tower of babble that we have for audio and video could be avoided by ensuring support for one container and one codec, neither of which are encumbered by patents or royalty requirements.

Find out more about the Ogg Vorbis container/codec at the official support site at *http://www.vorbis.com/*.

Apple and other companies, though, objected to the Ogg Vorbis requirement because of lack of hardware support, their belief that the Vorbis codec was inferior to other codecs, and concerns of potentially hidden patents (known as *submarine patents*) related to the codec.

Though the Xiph.Org foundation has done their best to search among patents to ensure Vorbis is patent free, there's no way to guarantee that unless it is challenged in a court of law. It's a catch-22 situation without any viable solution, so the section in the specification that required support for Ogg Vorbis was removed.

For an interesting historical perspective, the email from Ian Hickson, HTML5 editor, about dropping support for both Ogg Vorbis and Ogg Theara can be found online at *http://lists.whatwg.org/pipermail/whatwg -whatwg.org/2009-June/020620.html*.

Though Ogg Vorbis is no longer a requirement, several browsers do support it. Firefox, Opera, and Chrome support Ogg Vorbis, while Safari and IE do not.

The AAC Codec

The Advanced Audio Coding (AAC) lossy compression codec was originally considered to be a successor to MP3, though it didn't get broad acceptance. It languished, little known, until Apple picked it as the format for the files in its iTunes store. The container it's most used with is the MPEG-4 Part 14 container, known as MP4 for the .mp4 file extension. Though most of us assume that MP4 files are video, they can be audio only. In fact, another common file extension used with MP4 audio files is .m4a, again primarily because of Apple's influence. Safari, Chrome, and IE support MPEG-4 AAC.

WebM Audio

WebM is a container based on the profile for the Matroska Multimedia Container. WebM was designed from the beginning to be patent and royalty free. Google was instrumental in forming the organization behind WebM, but has given up any and all patent claims to the container.

Codec support in WebM is quite simple: WebM only supports Vorbis for audio, and VP8 for video (which I'll cover in the next section). The reasons for such simple codec support are given in a FAQ at the WebM web site:

> We decided to define WebM files in this way because we wanted to do what's best for users. Users just want video to work, they don't want to worry about supported codecs, file formats, and so on. After much discussion with browser makers, tool developers and others, we reached a consensus that a narrowly defined format would cause the least confusion for users. If a user has a *.webm* file, he or she can be confident that it will play in any browser or media player that supports WebM.

WebM is supported by Chrome, Firefox, and Opera. It is not currently supported by IE and Safari. However, people can ensure that WebM files work in their IE9 browser by installing the WebM plug-in for IE9 (found at *http://tools.google.com/dlpage/ webmmf*). However, since we as page authors, designers, and developers can't be sure that the WebM plug-in is installed, we have to provide support for browsers that currently don't support WebM.

 People typically think that WebM is solely a video file format. However, you can create a WebM file that consists of only one Vorbis data stream, and it works in an audio element. The source element's type setting is *audio/webm*. Find out more about WebM at the project website, at *http://www.webmproject.org/*.

I've covered the popular audio and video file types, but how do browsers know if an MP4 is an audio file, or a video file? Of if this file is an Ogg, and that is a WebM? Well, they can open the file and see for themselves. Or we can provide the information directly in the media element.

Providing Codec information in the type attribute

Earlier, I stated that an MP4 file can be audio or video. So how does the browser or other application know which type of file it is? Or what codec is being used in the MP4 container? In fact, what codec is used in any of the containers?

One approach is to use a popular and unique file extension, such as.m4a, and then add a MIME type to your web server for the extension. You can add the MIME type directly to the *mime.types* file for an Apache server, or you can add a MIME type to the directory's *.htaccess* file (assuming you're running Linux):

```
AddType audio/mp4 m4a
AddType video/ogg ogg oga
AddType video/webm webm
```

You should also use the **type** attribute in the source element. The **type** attribute provides information to the browsers and other user agents about the container and codec, as well as type of file listed in the **src** attribute. The syntax for the **type** attribute is the type of file, followed by the type of container. In Example 1-4, the container and media file type for each audio file is added to each of four **source** elements.

Example 1-4. HTML5 web page with embedded audio element with four separate audio types, each with their specific MIME type provided in the source element's type attribute

```
<!DOCTYPE html>
<head>
<title>Audio</title>
<meta charset="utf-8" />

</head>
<body>
<audio controls>
   <source src="audiofile.mp3" type="audio/mpeg" />
   <source src="audiofile.ogg" type="audio/ogg" />
   <source src="audiofile.wav" type="audio/wav" />
</audio>
</body>
```

Of course the last file, the WAV, never gets played, at least not with our target browsers. IE, Chrome, and Safari pick up the MP3, while Firefox and Opera pick up the Ogg file. Each browser traverses the source elements until if finds a file it can play, and then stops. Minimally, you can provide an MP3 and an Ogg or WebM audio file, which covers all five target browsers, in addition to iOS and Android.

Table 1-2 contains a summary of the different audio codecs and containers covered, as well as modern browser support, common file extension(s), and **type** setting.

Table 1-2. Audio container/codec support across popular modern browser versions

Container/Codec	Type	Extension(s)	IE9+	Firefox	Safari 5+	Chrome	Opera 11+
WAV	audio/wav or audio/wave	.wav	No	Yes	Yes	Yes	Yes
MP3	audio/mpeg	.mp3	Yes	No	Yes	Yes	No
Ogg Vorbis	audio/ogg	.ogg, .oga	No	Yes	No	Yes	Yes
MPEG-4 AAC	audio/mp4	.m4a	Yes	No	Yes	Yes	No
WebM Vorbis	audio/webm	.webm	No	Yes	No	Yes	Yes

HTML5 Video Element Codecs/Containers

As I mentioned in the last section, video files are far too large to serve up in anything other than a lossy compressed format. As with audio codecs, no one video codec works in all browsers.

H.264

One of the most popular lossy video codecs is MPEG-4 Part 10, commonly known as H.264. H.264 is a high quality, popular format that's common on the Internet and supported in YouTube and iTunes. It is also one of the three mandatory codecs supported by Blu-Ray players. It's a mature codec, first standardized by the MPEG group in 2003. H.264 is also a controversial choice because of the patents held on the codec by the organization, MPEG-LA. Though video files encoded in H.264 that are distributed without cost aren't subject to royalties, tools that encode or decode H.264 do have to pay royalties. The cost for these royalties is usually passed on to the tool buyer.

The H.264 video codec is combined with either the AAC or MP3 audio codec in an MPEG-4 container. This combination is typically known as MP4, and files are usually given an .mp4 extension . You'll also see files with .m4v extensions for H.264. Apple iTunes uses the .m4v extension with its videos, but they're also encumbered by DRM and won't play in HTML5 video elements.

The H.264 codec is the only video codec that Microsoft supports for IE. It's also supported by Safari. Chrome has dropped support for H.264, and Firefox and Opera have never supported it because of the patent issues.

Ogg Theora

Firefox, Opera, and Chrome do support another codec, Theora, from the same organization (Xiph.Org) that provided the Ogg container and Vorbis audio codec described in the last section. The Ogg Theora container/codec was originally the mandatory codec and container for video elements in HTML5 until Apple and other companies objected to the restriction. Neither IE nor Safari support Ogg Theora, though there are plug-ins that can be installed to provide support in both browsers.

Xiph.Org provides a plug-in that enables support for the Theora and Vorbis codecs in QuickTime, which indirectly enables support for Safari. Access the plug-in at *http://www.xiph.org/quicktime/about.html*. Another plug-in, OpenCodecs, provides more generalized support for Ogg Vorbis, Ogg Theora, WebM, and various other Ogg container/codec pairings, and can be accessed at *http://xiph.org/dshow/downloads/*.

WebM

The last video container I'll cover is WebM, which I introduced in the section on audio codecs. Unlike many of the other containers, WebM supports only one audio codec, Vorbis, and one video codec, VP8. VP8 was created by a company named On2, which was later bought by Google—who promptly open-sourced the VP8 codec.

WebM is supported by Chrome, Firefox, and Opera. There is no built-in support for WebM in Safari and IE, but, as mentioned earlier, there is plug-in support for WebM for both browsers.

Since Chrome, Firefox, and Opera support both Ogg Theora and WebM, which should you use? The answer is: it depends.

Both should continue to be supported for the foreseeable future. The Open Source community, including Wikipedia, still primarily support Ogg Theora, but since Google open-sourced VP8, this may change in the future. VP8 is generally considered a better codec than Theora, but I've never seen much difference in quality when it comes to videos sized and optimized for the web. But then, I'm not a picky videophile, either.

HTML5 and Streaming

HTML5 media elements are protocol agnostic, which means you can specify streaming audio and video in **audio** and **video**. The real issue with using streaming media is user agent and operating system support. As an example, Safari on the Mac Desktop supports Real-Time Streaming Protocol (RTSP), but Safari on iOS only supports HTTP Live Streaming. However, if you try to open an RTSP streaming video in Safari on Windows (from the YouTube mobile site at *m.youtube.com*), you'll get a protocol error (the same error you'll get with other browsers).

However, if you install an application such as Real Player to view the RTSP file, the file opens in the Real Player, rather than the browser. Streaming media support in HTML5 is definitely not for the faint of heart at this time.

Ensuring Complete Video Codec Support

You can't assume your web page readers have plug-ins installed to play Ogg or WebM videos in Safari or IE. In order to ensure that a video is accessible by all of the target browsers, you'll need to provide, at minimum, two different **source** elements for your video element. Example 1-5 shows an HTML5 web page with a video element containing two different video sources: one in H.264 (necessary for IE and Safari), and one in WebM (for Firefox, Opera, and Chrome). In addition, if you want to ensure that non-HTML5 compliant browsers have access to the video, you'll also need to provide some form of fallback. In the example below, the fallback is a YouTube video. Another choice can be Flash or another plug-in.

Example 1-5. HTML5 web page with video that works in all target browsers

```
<!DOCTYPE html>
<head>
    <title>Big Buck Bunny Video</title>
    <meta http-equiv="Content-Type" content="text/html;charset=utf-8" />
</head>
<body>
    <video controls>
        <source src="videofile.mp4" type="video/mp4" />
        <source src="videofile.webm" type="video/webm" />
        <iframe width="640" height="390"
            src="http://www.youtube.com/embed/YE7VzlLtp-4">
        </iframe>
    </video>
</body>
```

Figure 1-2 shows the video playing in Chrome, which supports the embedded HTML5 video. Figure 1-3 shows a YouTube video playing in IE9 with compatibility mode turned on, emulating an older version of IE that doesn't support HTML5 video.

 If you're unsure how to structure the fallback content in the video element to ensure access to the video in all user agents and browsers, I recommend reading Kroc Camen's article, "Video for Everybody", at *http://camendesign.com/code/video_for_everybody*.

Table 1-3 provides a summary of coverage of the three video codecs I covered in this section.

Table 1-3. Video container/codec support across popular modern browser versions

Container/Codec	Type	Extension(s)	IE9+	Firefox	Safari 5+	Chrome	Opera 11+
MP4+H.264+AAC	video/mp4	.mp4, .m4v	Yes	No	Yes	No	No
Ogg+Theora+Vorbis	video/ogg	.ogg, .ogv	No	Yes	No	Yes	Yes

Figure 1-2. Video playing in Chrome with support for HTML5 video

Figure 1-3. Video playing in IE9 in compatibility mode, triggering the YouTube fallback

Before I return to the media elements, there is one more attribute supported on the source element, though it is rarely used: the media attribute. The media attribute provides the intended media source for the element. The default value is *all*, which means the media file is intended for all media sources. There are several other allowable values, but the two that make most sense (other than *all*) for media elements, especially video, are *handheld* and *screen*. In combination with *media queries* in CSS, one can have a web page serve both desktop and handheld devices.

MPEG-LA and the VP8 Challenge

An interesting sidenote about WebM VP8 is the MPEG-LA group's announcement of the forming of a *patent pool* about the VP8 codec, not long after Google open-sourced the codec. Right after the MPEG-LA announcement, the US Justice Department opened an investigation into whether the MPEG-LA's effort violates trust law by attempting to sow uncertainty about WebM and VP8 and thus harm a potential competitor.

The MPEG-LA announcement of the formation of a patent pool can be read at *http://www.mpegla.com/main/pid/vp8/default.aspx*. More on the Justice Department's efforts can be read in an article at the Guardian, "US Justice Department reportedly investigating MPEG-LA over VP8 threats", online at *http://www.guardian.co.uk/technology/blog/2011/mar/04/justice-department-antitrust-mpeg-la-vp8*.

However, I'm not overly fond of trying to get one page to work in two completely different environments. Many sites have a mobile only version of the content, usually designated with a m subdirectory setting (such as *http://m.burningbird.net*). In the end, it may be simpler just to provide the separately formatted sites—especially with Content Management Systems (CMS) that serve all of the contents from a database.

 Drupal, the CMS I use, has a custom module named Domain Access (available at *http://drupal.org/project/domain*), that allows us to designate a different theme, page and content structure for pages served up with the *m* subdomain. Most other CMS tools offer something comparable.

The Media Elements in More Detail

After that refreshingly simple jaunt through containers and codecs, we'll return to looking at the media elements in more detail.

Media Elements and Global Attributes

The audio and video elements both support the same set of global attributes:

accesskey
> A unique, ordered, and space separated (as well as case sensitive) set of tokens that enables specifically named keyboard key access to the media element.

class
> A set of space separated tokens specifying the various classes the element belongs to.

contenteditable
> If true, content can be edited; if false, content cannot be edited.

contextmenu
> The id of the context menu associated with the element.

dir
> The directionality of the element's text.

draggable
> Whether the media element can be dragged. If true, the element can be dragged; if false, the element cannot be dragged.

dropzone
> What happens when an item is dropped on the element.

hidden
> A boolean attribute that determines if the element is "relevant". Elements that are hidden are not rendered.

id
> A unique identifier for the element.

lang
> Specifies the primary language of the element's contents.

spellcheck
> Set to true for enabling spell and grammar checking on the element's contents.

style
> Inline CSS styling.

tabindex
> Determines if media element is focusable, and the element's order is in the tabbing sequence.

title
> Advisory information, such as a tooltip.

data-*
> Custom data type, such as data-myownuse or data-thisappsuse. Used to read and write custom data values for use in your own applications.

Of course, not all of the global attributes seem relevant with both of the media elements. For instance, I can't see how it is possible to spell or grammar check the contents of a video. Others, though, are very useful.

If you need to access a specific audio or video element using JavaScript, you'll need to set its id attribute. You can capture an entire set of media elements in a page, and pinpoint the specific one you want by its page position, but it's easier just to use id.

If you have more than one media element on possibly different web pages, and you want to provide the same CSS styling for each, you'll need to assign a class for each, and then use the class name in your CSS stylesheet.

Being able to drag and drop media elements is a viable web action, so the draggable and dropzone attributes are useful. So are the accesskey and tabindex attributes if you want finer control over the element's keyboard access.

The hidden attribute may not seem as viable at first. However, you could use it to remove an audio or video element from rendering, while still ensuring access to the contents for purposes that don't depend on immediate reader access.

Media-Specific Attributes

In addition to the global attributes, there are also several media-specific attributes that are shared by both the audio and video elements. We've seen the src and controls attributes used in previous examples. The rest are provided in the following list:

preload

> The preload attribute provides hints to the user agent about preloading the media content. By hints, I mean that hopefully the user agent follows the directive, but may or may not. The acceptable values are *none*, which hints to hold on preloading the media until the user presses the play button (or otherwise wants the video to load); *metadata*, which hints to load the media's metadata only; or *auto*, the default state, which hints to the user agent to go ahead and download the resource.

autoplay

> The autoplay attribute is a boolean attribute whose presence signals the user agent to begin playing the media file as soon as it has loaded enough of the media file so that it can play through it without stopping. If autoplay is added to a media element, it overrides the preload setting, regardless of setting.

loop

> The loop attribute resets the media file back to the beginning when finished, and continues the play.

muted

> If the muted attribute is present, the media plays, but without sound. The user can turn on the sound via the media controls, if they wish.

mediagroup

The mediagroup attribute provides a way to group more than one media file together.

At the time this was written, the new mediagroup attribute had not been implemented by any browser. According to the specifications, if the attribute is provided for two or more media elements, they'll all be managed by the same implicitly created *media controller*. We can assume from the documentation that if one of the media files is played, the others are kept in sync. This behavior could be very helpful in situations such as having a video of a speech in one element, and a sign language interpretation of the speech in another element, or for emulating picture-in-picture with two videos.

The muted attribute is also extremely new, and had not been implemented—as an attribute—in any browser when this was written.

The combination of loop and autoplay can be used to create a background sound for when a page is loaded. You'll want to use this functionality sparingly, but it could be useful if you're creating a more presentation-like website where sound is tolerated, even expected, by your web page readers. Example 1-6 demonstrates how to use these attributes with an audio element that doesn't have a controls attribute, and is also hidden using CSS, just in case the user's browser has scripting disabled. The sound will play as soon as the page and media are loaded, and continue to play until the user leaves the page.

Example 1-6. A repeating auto started audio file in two different formats to ensure browser coverage

```
<!DOCTYPE html>
<head>
   <title>Repeating Audio</title>
   <meta charset="utf-8" />
   <style>
     #background
     {
         display: none;
     }
   </style>
</head>
<body>
   <audio id="background" autoplay loop>
      <source src="audiofile.mp3" type="audio/mpeg" />
      <source src="audiofile.ogg" type="audio/ogg" />
   </audio>
</body>
```

The example works in IE, Opera, Chrome, and Safari. It only partially worked in Firefox at the time this was written because Firefox (5, 6, or 7) doesn't currently support the loop attribute.

You'll want to use *display: none* for the CSS style setting of the audio element, to ensure that the element doesn't take up page space. You might be tempted to use the hidden attribute, but doing so just to hide the element is an inappropriate use of the attribute. The hidden attribute is meant to be used with material that isn't relevant immediately, but may be at some later time.

You can use the loop and autoplay with video files, but unless the video file is quite small, or encoded to load progressively, you're not going to get the same instant effect that you get with audio files.

Video-Only Attributes and Video Resolutions

There are a couple of attributes that are only specific to the video element.

poster
> The poster attribute is a way of providing a static image to display in the video element until the web page reader plays the video.

width, height
> The width and height attributes set the width and height of the video element. The control will resize to fit the video when it's played, but if the video is larger than the control, it pushes content out of the way and can be quite distracting to web page readers. If the video is smaller than the control, it's centered within the space.

The actual width and height of a video are directly related to the resolution of the video. If you have a Standard Definition (SD) video, you have a video that's 480 pixels in height (480 lines). If you have an HD video, you have a video that's 720 lines (pixels) tall, or taller. You can find the exact frame dimensions using a tool such as Handbrake (covered later in the chapter).

The poster and the width and height attributes imply that you know the size of the video. You'll want to provide the same size poster image as the video, and you'll want to size the control the same as a frame in the video. Providing both attributes ensures that your video presentation is smooth and polished, rather than other page content abruptly being pushed down as the video element automatically expands.

Example 1-7 shows a web page with a video element and two source elements that has the width, height, and poster attributes set.

Example 1-7. Video with the width and height set, as well as a poster image to display

```
<!DOCTYPE html>
<head>
   <title>Birdcage</title>
   <meta charset="utf-8" />
</head>
<body>
   <video controls width="640" height="480" poster="birdcageposter.jpg">
      <source src="birdcage.mp4" type="video/mp4" />
      <source src="birdcage.webm" type="video/webm" />
   </video>
</body>
```

The video controls are placed over the content, including the poster image, so place text in the poster image accordingly. In addition, Safari and IE seem to hide the poster image once the video has been fully cached, but Firefox, Opera, and Chrome will redisplay the poster image when the page is refreshed, even with the video cached, as shown in Chrome in Figure 1-4.

Figure 1-4. Video playing in Chrome with a poster image and width and height set, after video is fully cached

Regardless of how browsers handle the `width`, `height`, and `poster` attributes, their use increases the polished perception of the video.

Audio and Video in Mobile Devices and Media Profiles

Support for HTML5 audio and video, especially video, in mobile devices is varied and can be challenging for web page authors and designers.

Challenges of a Mobile Environment

There are known quirks about the use of the HTML5 media elements in mobile devices. For instance, Apple has been a big fan of HTML5 from the beginning, deciding against support for Flash on iOS devices in favor of HTML5 video. However, some things that work on the desktop don't in an Apple mobile environment. As an example, using the `poster` attribute caused the `video` element to fail in iOS 3, though this problem has been fixed in iOS 4. Another interesting little quirk was iPad's only checking the first `source` element, so you needed to place the MP4 video first in the list (again, since corrected).

In addition, the iOS environment has its own native application for playback control, so it ignores the `controls` attribute.

Then there are the issues of how to test your HTML5 media applications. Most of us can't afford to buy half a dozen devices (some of us can't afford to buy any) and emulators don't really work when it comes to testing out hardware and resource limitations.

 A good article on the issues of mobile testing is "Testing Apps For SmartPhones and Mobile Devices (Without Buying Out the Store)" at *http://www.softwarequalityconnection.com/2011/03/testing-apps-for -smartphones-and-mobile-devices-without-buying-out-the-store/*.

Most importantly, the video capability itself is limited in mobile environments. There is the resolution/size issue, of course, but there are also issues with containers and codecs. Mobile devices don't have the processing power our computers have, which means that the file sizes are larger (because of simpler compression techniques). At the same time, mobile devices have data access limitations as well as issues with storage, so larger files aren't mobile-friendly.

There's also the challenge associated with the sheer number of mobile operating systems, mobile browsers, and devices—especially devices.

At this time, the iOS supports H.264, and the Android OS supports H.264 and WebM (though without hardware acceleration). Since Google is making a move away from H.264, we can assume the Android OS will, eventually, drop support for H.264. Maybe. In addition, the upcoming release of Windows Phone 7 from Microsoft, codenamed "Mango", supposedly includes support for HTML5 video. Since Windows Phone 7 is Microsoft, we have to assume it will have H.264 support. Nokia is transitioning to Windows Phone 7, but is not offering HTML5 video and audio in its next release of its built-in Symbian operating system. However, you can run Opera Mobile on Symbian/S60, and get HTML5 video and audio support. Opera supports only Ogg and WebM. Blackberry supports H.264 video, but not the HTML5 `video` element—you'll have to use a link.

What we can take away from all of this is that to support mobile devices, you'll need to provide appropriately sized video files, as well as include support for both WebM/Ogg Theora and H.264. But not just any H.264. You need to provide videos encoded with the right *profile*.

Media Profiles and Codec Parameters

Since H.264 was designed to meet the needs of large television sets to small mobile phones, H.264 incorporates a concept known as a *profile*. Each profile defines a set of optional features, balanced against the file size. The more the video relies on the hardware, the smaller the file size. H.264 supports 17 profiles, but the ones we're interested in are *baseline*, *main*, *extended*, and *high*. As you would expect, the hardware requirements for each increases from *baseline* to *high*.

Different devices support different protocols. Microsoft supports all H.264 profiles, but Safari only supports the *main* profile, because that's all QuickTime supports by default. Mobile devices, such as those running iOS and the Android OS, run the *baseline* profile. If your site needs to provide both mobile and larger videos, you may want to encode several versions with different H.264 videos. It's actually simple to ensure the right encoding, because most conversion tools provide device profile presets (more on this later in the chapter).

 The WHATWG Wiki provides a page giving several different type codec parameters, at *http://wiki.whatwg.org/wiki/Video_type_parameters*.

In order to ensure that each device knows which video works best for it (without having to load the video's metadata and extract the information), you can provide the information directly in the source element's type attribute. An example of the syntax to use is the following, for an Ogg Theora video file:

```
<source src='videofile.ogg' type='video/ogg; codecs="theora, vorbis"' />
```

The syntax is container first, then the codecs in video, audio order.

The codec specification for WebM is as simple as Ogg, but the same cannot be said for H.264 because of all of the profile possibilities. The audio codec is low-level AAC (*mp4a.40.2*), but the video codec is profile and level based. From the WHATWG Wiki that collects the type parameters, the video codec for H.264 can be any one of the five following codecs:

- H.264 Baseline: avc1.42E0xx, where xx is the AVC level
- H.264 Main: avc1.4D40xx, where xx is the AVC level
- H.264 High: avc1.6400xx, where xx is the AVC level

- MPEG-4 Visual Simple Profile Level 0: mp4v.20.9
- MPEG-4 Visual Advanced Simple Profile Level 0: mp4v.20.240

The profile part is easy, because when you use conversion tools, most have presets predefined for each of the profiles. However, the AVC level isn't as simple to discover. According to a paper on H.264 (a PDF is available at *http://www.fastvdo.com/spie04/ spie04-h264OverviewPaper.pdf*), the AVC level is based on picture size and framework, and also added constraints for picture number reference and compression rate.

In Example 1-8, several different video files are listed in individual source elements, with both the codec and container information in the type attribute. The two H.264 videos represent a desktop capable video encoded with the *main* profile, while the mobile version is encoded with the *baseline* profile. The user agent in each environment traverses the list of source elements, stopping when it reaches a container/codec and profile it supports.

Example 1-8. Several video sources, each with different container/codec strings in the source type attribute

```
<!DOCTYPE html>
<head>
   <title>Video</title>
   <meta charset="utf-8" />
</head>
<body>
   <video controls>
      <source src="videofile.mp4"
              type='video/mp4; codecs="codecs="avc1.4D401E, mp4a.40.2"' />
      <source src="videofilemobile.mp4"
              type='video/mp4; codecs="avc1.42E01E, mp4a.40.2"' />
      <source src="videofile.webm"
              type='video/webm; codecs="vp8, vorbis"' />
      <source src="videofile.ogv"
              type='video/ogg, codecs="theora, vorbis"' />
   </video>
</body>
```

 The Android Developer SDK documentation contains a listing of supported media types and recommended encodings at *http://developer.an droid.com/guide/appendix/media-formats.html*. The iOS Developer Library has a "Getting Started" section for audio and video at *http://devel oper.apple.com/library/ios/#referencelibrary/GettingStarted/GS_Audio Video_iPhone/_index.html*. The announcement of an integrated IE9 into Windows Phone 7, including HTML5 media support, can be found at *http://blogs.msdn.com/b/ie/archive/2011/02/14/ie9-on-windows-phone .aspx*.

Converting Audio and Video Content

I have a little Flip video camera that I use to take videos. It's a cute little thing, and easy to use. Unfortunately, it's been discontinued because so many smart phones have built-in video capability that meets or exceeds the Flip's capability.

My Flip, and most video phones and other cameras, take video in the MP4 format. In addition, most of our devices now support HD video, which means large video files that may or may not be useful for web access. Once you have a video—your own, or a CC or public domain video you found online—you need to provide conversions of the video for all of your target browsers and environments. This means, on average, creating smaller or edited versions of the video, and converting the resulting video into either Ogg or WebM format (or H.264 if the video is a WAV or other video format).

In addition, you may have a WMA (Windows Media Audio) file that doesn't play on the web, which you need to convert into a web-friendly format.

The number of tools to edit both audio and video files can fill a book, so I'll leave that for another book. Instead I'm going to introduce you to some useful tools you can use to create video and audio conversions for various browsers and environments.

The Free Mp3/Wma/Ogg Converter

The tool I used for most of the audio conversions for this book is the Free Mp3/Wma/ Ogg Converter, by Cyberpower. This tool is extremely easy to use, and can convert one audio file or do batch conversions.

 Download the Free Mp3/Wma/Ogg Converter from *http://www .freemp3wmaconverter.com/*.

When you start the tool, you're presented with a blank workspace, and buttons to the right for adding source video files. The tool can work with Ogg Vorbis, WMA, and MP3 source files, and you can add more than one source file, as shown in Figure 1-5.

Clicking the Next button at the bottom of the window leads to the next page, where you can select from several audio output formats. For instance, you can pick from a list of Ogg Vorbis quality conversion choices, as shown in Figure 1-6.

Figure 1-5. Adding files for conversion to the Free Mp3/Wma/Ogg audio converter

Figure 1-6. Selecting Ogg container and Vorbis codec, as well as quality in Free Mp3/Wma/Ogg converter

Video Conversion with Miro Video Converter and Handbrake

For video, I use two different tools: Miro Video Converter, and Handbrake.

The Miro Video Converter is even simpler to use than Free Mp3/Wma/Ogg. When you open the application, you have a space where you can either drag a file for conversion, or open the utility to find the file, as shown in Figure 1-7.

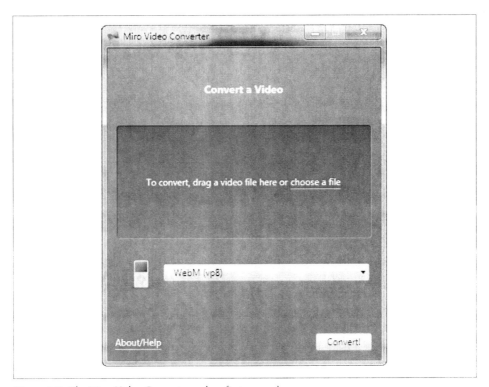

Figure 1-7. The Miro Video Converter, when first opened

After loading a source file, you then pick which container and profile you want the video file to be converted to. In Figure 1-8, I've selected the Android Droid preset.

It can take a little time to do the conversion, depending on how much juice your machine has. However, the simplicity of the conversion process makes it an ideal tool for those just getting started.

If you want a little more sophistication with H.264 files, I recommend Handbrake. It doesn't do any conversions to WebM or Ogg, but it does give you more finite control over your H.264 conversion, especially for web content.

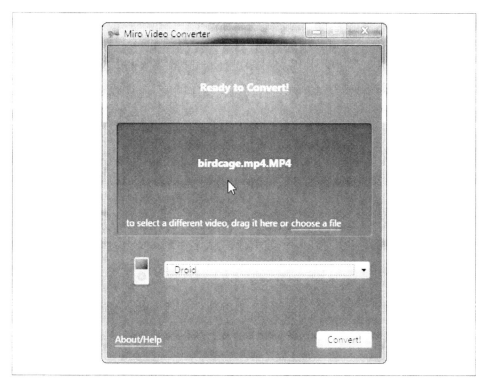

Figure 1-8. After selecting the Android Droid preset in Miro Video Converter

 The Miro Video Converter can be found at *http://www.mirovideo converter.com/*. Downloads and documentation for Handbrake can be found at *http://handbrake.fr/*.

Once you start up Handbrake, you'll need to provide a source file. This can be a DVD (unless protected), or it can be a video file or folder, as shown in Figure 1-9. In the figure, the source file is the Ogg Theora 854 × 480 video of Big Buck Bunny.

At this point you can choose a preset in the right column, or you can manually choose your settings from several different tab pages. For instance, you can set the video resolution (width and height) and aspect ratio in the first tab page, and in the tab page labeled "Video" you can pick the framerate and bitrate, as well as selecting the 2 pass encoding option. You can adjust the audio in the tab page labeled "Audio", and add subtitles via the tab page labeled "Subtitles". If you want to provide closed captioning within the file, this is where you'll add the subtitles. You can even choose to "burn in" the subtitles if you want them to be available for everyone.

Figure 1-9. Loading an Ogg Theora source video file into Handbrake

For the sample, I picked the *iPhone & iPod Touch* preset. Doing so removed some options, such as the 2 pass Encoding, which I would normally pick if the preset allows it (or I was manually setting all of the encoding values). I also checked the *Web Optimized* option, which means that the video loads progressively (the video can start playing before it's completely loaded.) Always, always, pick the *Web Optimized* option if the file is meant for HTML5 video access.

Figure 1-10 shows the front page of Handbrake during the encoding process.

Using a Frame Grabber

One last tool I used for the book is a *frame grabber*. Frame grabbers allow you to traverse through your video file while the video is running, or frame by frame, or both. You can then grab a static copy of whatever frame interests you. I used the freely available Avidemux as a frame grabber (though it does more than just grab frames), to get a static image for the `poster` attribute example earlier in the chapter.

 You can download Avidemux and access the Wiki documents at *http:// avidemux.sourceforge.net/*.

Figure 1-10. During the conversion of the Ogg Theora file to MP4 using Handbrake

Once Avidemux is opened, select and open your video file. Unless the frame is close to the beginning of the file, click the play button to run the video to the approximate place in the video for the frame you're interested in. Stop the video, and then use the frame buttons to move forwards or backwards, a frame at a time, to find the frame you want, as shown in Figure 1-11.

Once you have the frame you want in the viewfinder, select the File menu option, then the Save and Save JPEG menu options, and give the tool a location and file name for the grabbed frame in the dialog that opens. Avidemux only saves frames as BMP or JPEG, but the JPEG should be sufficient for a frame that you want to use as a `poster` image for your video.

Once you have your static frame copy, you can then edit it in your favorite image editor, and add text or other effects. Even though the file is a JPEG, and a lossy compression format, opening the file once, adding effects, and saving a new copy won't degrade the copy enough to be noticeable.

There are dozens of tools for every environment for creating, editing, and converting audio, video, or both. My recommendation is try out several to see which ones work for you. Once you have your files, and your basic HTML5 (including all of the containers/codecs you want to support), check out what you can do with HTML5 audio and video out of the box, in Chapter 2.

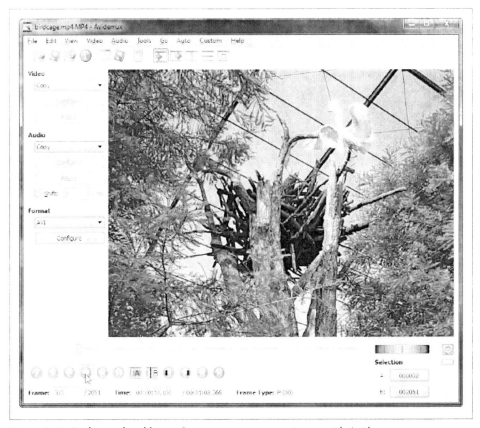

Figure 1-11. Finding and grabbing a frame to use as a poster image with Avidemux

 Mark Pilgrim provides excellent coverage of the HTML5 media elements, the codecs (and their related issues), as well as tools—including some open source command line tools good for batch processing— either in his book, HTML5: Up and Running (O'Reilly), or freely available at *http://diveintohtml5.org/video.html*.

CHAPTER 2

Customizing Media Elements

In Chapter 1, we looked at HTML5 audio and video in the box. In this chapter, we'll look at how we can customize the elements.

We'll try our hands at customizing the appearance of the controls with CSS, first, and then creating a custom set of controls using CSS and JavaScript. We'll also explore, in-depth, the HTMLMediaElement—the core element that provides API support for both media elements.

Lastly, I'll demonstrate how to use the browser debugger tools in order to determine exactly what each browser currently supports with the HTML5 media element.

The HTML5 web page we'll use as the base for all of the examples is given in Example 2-1. No fallback content is shown, in order to keep the examples as clean as possible.

Example 2-1. A basic, conformingHTML5 web page with a video element, with three different source elements

```
<!DOCTYPE html>
<head>
    <title>video</title>
    <meta charset="utf-8" />
</head>
<body>
    <video controls width="480" height="270" poster="bigbuckposter.png">
        <source src="videofile.mp4" type="video/mp4" />
        <source src="videofile.webm" type="video/webm" />
    </video>
</body>
```

The examples in this chapter focus on the video element. However, many of the effects described in the chapter can be applied, equally, to both audio and video.

CSS Styling

Both HTML5 media elements are block elements. Think of them as div elements...with perks. However you can style a div element, you can style an audio or video element. The only difference between them, from a styling perspective, is the div element can contain other HTML elements, while the media elements can only contain the source and target elements.

 Any additional HTML contained in the media elements is fallback material accessible only to browsers that don't support the HTML5 media elements.

You can size the media elements, position them, hide or show them, change their opacity, add a background and border—many of the same CSS effects you can apply to div elements. You can even apply some of the very new CSS3 transform and transition effects.

Adding a Fancy Border

The HTML5 media elements are functional, but not necessarily attractive. The elements are a box that also has a display area if the element is a video. The media element controls are plain but intuitive. The controls also differ between browsers, and between operating systems.

There is little you can do to control the appearance of the media element controls currently at this time, but you can control the appearance of the media containers using standard CSS. For instance, you can add a nice border, a box shadow, even add an overlay. You can also combine CSS rules to create more complex effects.

Figure 2-1 shows one effect that combines the CSS border, border-radius, and linear-gradient properties to create a gently pink, rounded corner, gradient background for the video element, with a subtle box shadow to provide dimension.

To create this effect, add the CSS in Example 2-2 to the HTML5 page given in Example 2-1 at the beginning of the chapter.

Figure 2-1. Combining the linear-gradient, border-radius, and box-shadow properties to create a styled background for a video element.

Example 2-2. CSS style setting for video element to create effect shown in Figure 2-1.

```
<style>
   video
      {
      /* basic border */
      border: 1px solid #ccc;
      padding: 20px;
      margin: 10px;
      border-radius: 20px;

      /* add regular background */
      background-color: #ffcccc;

      /* add gradient background */
      background-image: -moz-linear-gradient(top, #fff, #fcc);
      background-image: -webkit-linear-gradient(top, #fff, #fcc);
      background-image: -o-linear-gradient(top, #fff, #fcc);
      background-image: -ms-linear-gradient(top, #fff, #fcc);
      background-image: linear-gradient(top, #fff, #fcc);
```

```
        /* now a shadow */
        -webkit-box-shadow: 0 0 10px #ccc;
        box-shadow: 0 0 10px #ccc;
        }
</style>
```

A fallback solid color is provided for user agents that don't yet support the `linear-gradient` property.

Speaking of which:

- Safari 5 does not support the new linear-gradient syntax, but Webkit Nightly does. Both support the `border-radius` and `box-shadow` properties if using the vendor-specific *-webkit-box-shadow*.
- Chrome 12 and up supports all of the properties.
- Firefox 5 and up also supports all of the properties.
- IE9 doesn't support the `linear-gradient` property, but does support the `border-radius` and `box-shadow` properties.
- IE10 supports all of the properties.
- Opera 11 and up supports all of the properties.

There isn't anything unique about the `video` element that requires any special CSS handling. The only reason the CSS style setting is so long is because of the necessity of providing the vendor-specific settings for the linear gradient, since this CSS style property hasn't been formalized in the W3C yet.

 The vendor-specific prefixes are -moz- for Mozilla/Firefox; -o- for Opera; -ms- for Microsoft/Internet Explorer; and -webkit- for Chrome and Safari. More on the gradients at *http://dev.w3.org/csswg/css3-images/*.

The non-vendor-specific setting given in the last line matches that of the current specification, and is added for future proofing of the stylesheet.

Using the CSS Pseudo Classes

The *CSS pseudo classes* also work with the media elements. For instance, the `:hover` and `:focus` pseudo classes can be used with the `video` element to provide feedback whenever the user moves the mouse cursor over the video file, or it gets focus because of keyboard activity. Adding the following CSS to the stylesheet defined in Example 2-2 creates a brighter pink glow around the video when the mouse cursor is over the element, or the element receives focus:

```
video:hover, video:focus
    {
    /* add glow */
    -webkit-box-shadow: 0 0 20px #f88;
    box-shadow: 0 0 20px #f88;
    }
```

Now, whenever the user moves their mouse over (or tabs to) the video element, a nice pink glow pops up, as shown in Figure 2-2.

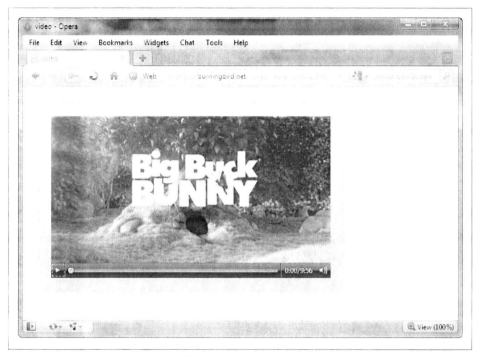

Figure 2-2. Providing a subtle visual effect, a pink glow, when the video element receives keyboard or mouse focus

Firefox, Opera, and IE currently support tabbing to the video element by default, but you'll need to add the tabindex attribute with Webkit-based browsers (Chrome and Safari):

```
<video controls width="480" height="270" poster="bigbuckposter.jpg"
    tabindex="0">
    <source src="videofile.mp4" type="video/mp4" />
    <source src="videofile.webm" type="video/webm" />
</video>
```

All the browsers support the CSS pseudo class effect.

Applying a CSS3 Transform to a Video Element

The new CSS3 transforms are a kick to work with, especially with active content such as the `video` element. There's no special processing you need in order to create media elements that get skewed, scaled, or otherwise twisted about.

Figure 2-3 shows the `video` element from earlier examples, except now it's been spun on its head, and scaled to one-half the size when the page is loaded.

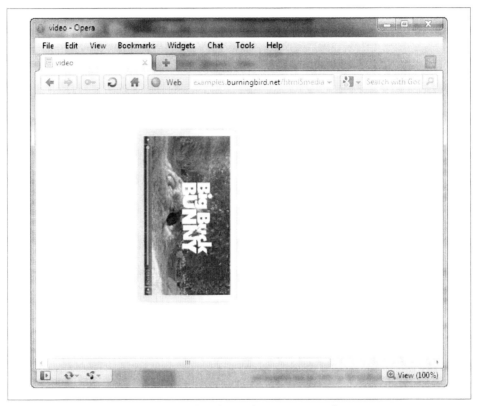

Figure 2-3. Video element scaled, rotated, and moved using CSS transforms

Once the video gets keyboard focus, or the mouse cursor moves over the element, then it returns to the default orientation and normal size. No JavaScript or other technology is used: it's all CSS—the CSS `transform` property, to be exact.

Some of you may be familiar with how CSS transforms work. If so, you can skip the next couple of paragraphs and go right to the code in Example 2-3.

The CSS3 2D transforms provide a way to manipulate HTML elements—including the media elements—in two-dimensional space. It doesn't matter how warped you make the media element, it still responds as a non-transformed media element.

All the transformations are functions on the CSS `transform` property. The functions include:

scale(number [, number])
> Scale the element, either by providing one value for both X and Y values, or two values (one for the X and one for the Y value).

scaleX(number), scaleY(number)
> Scale the element by the given number, either along the X value (scaleX), or the Y value (scaleY).

rotate(angle)
> Rotate the element by the angle about the origin.

skew(angle[,angle])
> Skew the element along both axes. If the second angle is not provided, the skew angle is the same for both the X and Y axis.

skewX(angle), skewY(angle)
> Skew the element along the respective axis.

translate(value[,value])
> Applying the translate transform effectively repositions the element, either by whole values or percentages, positive or negative values. If the second value is omitted, it's assumed to be zero.

translateX(value), translateY(value)
> Apply the translate transform, either in the X direction, or Y direction, accordingly.

matrix(val1, val2, val3, val4, val5, val6)
> The matrix transform is a way of combining all of the other transform effects into one transform function call.

The only other transformation is the `transform-origin` property, which modifies the origin for transformations for the element. For instance, when you rotate an element, the center of the transform is the center of the rotation. If you want to center the rotation at the element's left-top corner, you would use the following:

```
transform: rotate(30deg);
transform-origin: 0 0;
```

If you don't provide the `transform-origin`, the element shifts out of place during the rotation.

By default, `transform-origin` is set to a value of 50% 50%, but can be changed—either by providing one value (which sets the horizontal value, vertical is set to 50%); two values (setting both horizontal and vertical); using percentages (50% 50%) or actual values (-100px, 100px); or by providing named values (such as top, top center, or center top, which equates to values of 50% 0).

Example 2-3 replicates the stylesheet in Example 2-2, except that transforms are used when the element is first loaded, and again when the element gets keyboard or mouse focus. When first loaded, the video element is scaled one-half size, and rotated 90 degrees. It's also moved 100 pixels "up" the page, by translating it 100 pixels along the X axis (which is now the vertical axis since the element has been rotated). When it gets the focus, though, it's scaled back to normal size, returned to the normal rotation (0 degrees), and moved back to the default position.

Example 2-3. Applying CSS3 transforms to a video element

```
<style>
   video
      {
      /* basic border */
      border: 1px solid #ccc;
      padding: 20px;
      margin: 20px;
      border-radius: 20px;

      /* add regular background */
      background-color: #ffcccc;

      /* add gradient background */
      background-image: -moz-linear-gradient(top, #fff, #fcc);
      background-image: -webkit-linear-gradient(top, #fff, #fcc);
      background-image: -o-linear-gradient(top, #fff, #fcc);
      background-image: -ms-linear-gradient(top, #fff, #fcc);
      background-image: linear-gradient(top, #fff, #fcc);

      /* now a shadow */
      -webkit-box-shadow: 0 0 10px #ccc;
      box-shadow: 0 0 10px #ccc;

      /* now transform */
      -moz-transform: scale(0.5) translate(-100px, 0) rotate(90deg);
      -webkit-transform: scale(0.5) translate(-100px, 0) rotate(90deg);
      -o-transform: scale(0.5) translate(-100px, 0) rotate(90deg);
      -ms-transform: scale(0.5) translate(-100px, 0) rotate(90deg);
      transform: scale(0.5) translate(-100px, 0) rotate(90deg);
      }

   video:hover, video:focus
      {
      /* add glow */
      -webkit-box-shadow: 0 0 20px #f88;
      box-shadow: 0 0 20px #f88;

      /* rotate and move video */
      -moz-transform: scale(1.0) translate(0) rotate(0deg);
      -webkit-transform: scale(1.0) translate(0) rotate(0deg);
      -o-transform: scale(1.0) translate(0) rotate(0deg);
      -ms-transform: scale(1.0) translate(0) rotate(0deg);
      transform: scale(1.0) translate(0) rotate(0deg);
      }
</style>
```

I highlighted the changes in the example in bold to make them easier to spot. The transform works with all of the target browsers, including IE9. Be aware, though, that Safari 5 on Windows seems to be preoccupied with loading the video and may not immediately respond to the mouse hover or keyboard focus.

Figure 2-4 shows the `video` element when it receives the keyboard focus. It's a good thing the element accepts both the keyboard and mouse focus in order to return to normalcy, or you'd have to keep your mouse over the video just to watch it without having to turn your head to the side.

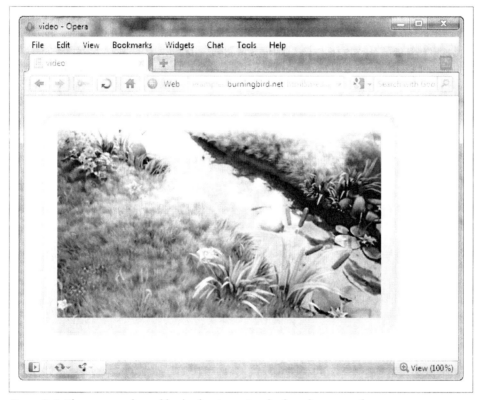

Figure 2-4. Element transformed back when it receives keyboard or mouse focus

 For more on the new CSS3 transforms, you can check out Mozilla's page on transforms at *https://developer.mozilla.org/en/css/-moz-trans form*. Opera also has a nice page on CSS transforms and transitions at *http://dev.opera.com/articles/view/css3-transitions-and-2d-transforms/*, as does Apple, found at *http://developer.apple.com/library/safari/#docu mentation/InternetWeb/Conceptual/SafariVisualEffectsProgGuide/ Transforms/Transforms.html*.

Animating the Transforms with CSS3 Transitions

I like the effect of rotating the video and scaling it larger when it gets focus. I can see using this if you have several videos you want to add to a page and have limited space. What I don't like, though, is that the fact that the transformation is so abrupt.

I'm not alone in this dislike of abrupt transitions. We've learned from our web page readers over the years that they would rather see a transition in action then to see an abrupt change. The transition shouldn't be too slow, but a suggestion of smooth movement that progresses from point A to point B seems to please the most people. However, creating these smooth transitions in the past using JavaScript has always been a rather daunting task.

Luckily, CSS3 again comes to the rescue with the transition properties. And, as with CSS transforms, CSS transitions work nicely with the media elements, including the video element.

 If you're already familiar with the CSS3 transition properties, you might want to skip to Example 2-5 at the end of this section. If you need more background on transitions, check out Mozilla's documentation on this new CSS functionality at *https://developer.mozilla.org/en/CSS/CSS_tran sitions*.

The CSS3 transition properties are:

transition-property
Acceptable values are *all*, *none*, or the CSS property being tracked, such as *opac ity* or *transform*. Choosing *all* applies the transition to any CSS property change.

transition-duration
Length of time a transition takes.

transition-timing-function
Used to determine the intermediate effects of the transition. Named values include *ease*, *linear*, *ease-in*, *ease-out*, and others.

transition-delay
When the transition will start.

transition
A shortcut that combines all of the above values.

The transition I use the most is the following, which enables the transition for all CSS properties, with a one second duration and using the *ease-in-out transition* timing function:

```
transition: all 1s ease-in-out
```

Since the transition properties haven't been formalized yet, vendor-specific settings need to be used. Example 2-4 shows the transition properties (highlighted) added to the stylesheet for the video element in the example we've been building on—enabling a nice, smooth transition between the rotated scaled video and the normal view.

Example 2-4. Adding the transition property to the existing style settings for the video element

```
video
  {
  /* basic border */
  border: 1px solid #ccc;
  padding: 20px;
  margin: 20px;
  border-radius: 20px;

  /* add regular background */
  background-color: #ffcccc;

  /* add gradient background */
  background-image: -moz-linear-gradient(top, #fff, #fcc);
  background-image: -webkit-linear-gradient(top, #fff, #fcc);
  background-image: -o-linear-gradient(top, #fff, #fcc);
  background-image: -ms-linear-gradient(top, #fff, #fcc);
  background-image: linear-gradient(top, #fff, #fcc);

  /* now a shadow */
  -webkit-box-shadow: 0 0 10px #ccc;
  box-shadow: 0 0 10px #ccc;

  /* now transform */
  -moz-transform: scale(0.5) translate(-100px, 0) rotate(90deg);
  -webkit-transform: scale(0.5) translate(-100px, 0) rotate(90deg);
  -o-transform: scale(0.5) translate(-100px, 0) rotate(90deg);
  -ms-transform: scale(0.5) translate(-100px, 0) rotate(90deg);
  transform: scale(0.5) translate(-100px, 0) rotate(90deg);

  /* set up transition */
  -webkit-transition: all 1s ease-in-out;
  -moz-transition: all 1s ease-in-out;
  -o-transition: all 1s ease-in-out;
  -ms-transition: all 1s ease-in-out;
  transition: all 1s ease-in-out;
  }
```

Since the transition property was added to the video element's stylesheet setting, and applies to any CSS property, any change to the video element CSS has a transition effect. This includes the transform, but also includes the change to the box shadow (from subtle gray to stronger, brighter pink). The transition works in all our target browsers except for IE—either IE9 or IE10.

> The specification for the CSS 2D Transform can be found at *http://www .w3.org/TR/css3-2d-transforms/*. The one for CSS Transitions is at *http: //www.w3.org/TR/css3-transitions/*.

Adding an Overlay

If CSS3 transforms and transitions are new kids that take some time to wrap our minds around, a simple overlay is an old web development friend. An overlay is just one element layered over the other—typically a div element layered over another element.

Developers who create custom controls for HTML media elements use overlays, but another use is to provide information about the video, such as producer, director, and so on. Example 2-5 demonstrates using an overlay to provide information about the Big Buck Bunny video when the video receives mouse or keyboard focus.

In the example, both the div element and the video share the same container. The container's CSS position property is set to *relative*, so that when the div element's position is set absolutely to *0,0*, it stays within the container. The div element is sized the same as the media element.

The div element contains information about the movie. It's "hidden" by default by setting the element's opacity to 0, making the element transparent. When a video receives focus, the overlay's opacity goes to 0.8, making it 80% opaque and therefore visible. When the video loses the focus, the overlay's opacity is again returned to 0. The video is set to autoplay when the page is loaded.

Example 2-5. A simple CSS-based overlay with the video element

```
<!DOCTYPE html>
<head>
   <title>video</title>
   <meta charset="utf-8" />
   <style>
      #container
      {
         position: relative;
      }
      #overlay
      {
         background-color: white;
         width: 480px;
         height: 270px;
         position: absolute;
         left: 0; top: 0;
         opacity: 0.0;

         /* set up transition */
         -webkit-transition: all 1s ease-in-out;
         -moz-transition: all 1s ease-in-out;
         -o-transition: all 1s ease-in-out;
         -ms-transition: all 1s ease-in-out;
         transition: all 1s ease-in-out;

      }
      #overlay:hover, #overlay:focus
```

```
        {
            opacity: 0.8;
        }

        #overlay h1, #overlay ul, #overlay p
        {
            margin: 10px;
        }
    </style>
</head>
<body>
    <div id="container">
        <video width="480" height="270" autoplay poster="bigbuckposter.jpg"
            tabindex="0" controls>
            <source src="videofile.mp4" type="video/mp4" />
            <source src="videofile.webm" type="video/webm" />
        </video>
        <div id="overlay">
            <h1>Big Buck Bunny</h1>
            <p>Another fine work from the Blender Institute</p>
            <ul>
                <li>Script and direction by: Sacha Goedegebure (Netherlands)</li>
                <li>Art direction: Andreas Goralczyk (Germany)</li>
                <li>Lead Artist: Enrico Valenza (Italy)</li>
                <li>Animation: Nathan Vegdahl (USA), William Reynish (Denmark)</li>
                <li>Technical directors: Brecht van Lommel (Belgium)
                    en Campbell Barton (Australia)</li>
                <li>Music by: Jan Morgenstern (Germany)</li>
                <li>Produced by: Ton Roosendaal (Netherlands)</li>
            </ul>
        </div>
    </div>
</body>
```

The overlay isn't completely opaque when the video element receives focus—we can still see the video through the text, though the text is very readable. In addition, the opacity of the overlay is incremented gradually using a CSS transition, which makes a nice effect. The overlay application works in all of our target browsers other than IE not supporting the transition effect.

The overlay is a technique that works without script, and works well...except for one problem. If you attempt to stop the video or pause it during play, you can't. Why? Because the overlay also hides the video controls. In order to use something like an overlay with a video element, what's needed is a way of providing a set of media controls that exist outside of the actual media element. For this functionality, though, we'll need JavaScript.

 Chapter 3 gets into more advanced manipulation of a video element's appearance, using SVG and the canvas element.

Custom Controls with JavaScript and CSS

One of the concerns people had about the media elements, right from the start, is the fact that you can't customize the controls using CSS. As the last section demonstrated, you can add borders and overlays (as well as transforms and transitions) to a media element, but you can't style the control buttons or even move the control independently of the media element.

Luckily, there is an option that provides this missing facility: using JavaScript, CSS, and the HTML media API (Application Programming Interface) to create and style custom media element controls.

Creating a Basic Control

User agents such as browsers that provide support for the HTML5 media elements also expose the HTMLMediaElement interface. This interface provides a set of methods, properties, and events that provide information about, as well as an ability to control, the media elements.

The HTMLMediaElement methods are given in Table 2-1.

Table 2-1. HTMLMediaElement Methods

Method	Purpose
canPlayType(string)	Checks the container type and codec information passed in the string to see if the user agent can play the type
load()	Begins loading the media content
pause()	Pauses playback
play()	Begins playback of the media content
addTextTrack(kind, label, language)	Creates and returns a MutableTextTrack object

The canPlayType method takes a string that contains the same string used with the type attribute discussed in Chapter 1. The syntax is container type, followed by the codec in video then audio order. An example with Ogg Theora is:

```
video/ogg; codecs="vp8, vorbis"
```

The canPlayType method returns one of three values:

probably
: If the user agent determines that it can probably play the media type

maybe
: If the user agent can't determine whether it can play the media file, until it actually tries to play it

empty string
> If the user agent knows for sure it can't play the media type

Interesting values, if a little vague. The method is handy, though, as a way of testing what user agent can play what media type. Example 2-6 shows an application that uses canPlayType with several different type strings to create a table browser codec support.

Example 2-6. Testing media types with the HTMLMediaElement canPlay method

```
<!DOCTYPE html>
<head>
   <title>video canplay</title>
   <meta charset="utf-8" />
   <style>
      td, table
         { border: 1px solid #ccc; }
      td
         { padding: 10px; }
   </style>
   <script>
      window.onload=function() {
         var videoElement = document.createElement("video");
         // load formats
         var formats =[
            'video/webm; codecs="vp8, vorbis"',
            'video/ogg; codecs="theora, vorbis"',
            'video/ogg; codecs="theora, speex"',
            'video/mp4; codecs="avc1.42E01E, mp4a.40.2"',
            'video/mp4; codecs="avc1.58A01E, mp4a.40.2"',
            'video/mp4; codecs="avc1.4D401E, mp4a.40.2"',
            'video/mp4; codecs="avc1.64001E, mp4a.40.2"',
            'video/mp4; codecs="mp4v.20.8, mp4a.40.2"',
            'video/mp4; codecs="mp4v.20.240, mp4a.40.2"'];

         // build support table
         var results = "<table><tr><th>Container/Codec</th><th>CanPlay</th>";
         for (var i = 0; i < formats.length; i++) {
            var result = videoElement.canPlayType(formats[i]);

            // if empty string, convert to dashed string
            if (result.length <= 0) result = "----";

            // add row
            results+="<tr><td>" + formats[i] + "</td><td>" +
                  result + "</td></tr>";
         }
         results+="</table>";

         // append to page
         document.getElementById("results").innerHTML=results;
      }
   </script>
</head>
<body>
   <h1>What can your browser play?</h1>
```

```
    <div id="results"></div>
</body>
```

The results of opening the page in various browsers are what we would expect from the discussions of codec support in Chapter 1:

- Opera and Firefox answer *probably* for the WebM and Ogg Theora video types, and return an empty string for every other media type
- Internet Explorer answers *probably* for the four H.264 profiles, and an empty string for all other types
- Safari answers *probably* for the four H.264 and the two MPEG-4 Visual Simple and Advanced types
- Chrome is the only user agent that just doesn't want to say no—answering *probably* for the Ogg Theora and WebM types, and also the four H.264 types, and *maybe* for everything else.

The other HTMLMediaElement methods can be used to create a custom control. We'll also need at least one of the HTMLMediaElement properties, currentTime. It and the other HTMLMediaElement properties are listed in Table 2-2. As you can quickly see, the HTMLMediaElement interface is a busy little creature.

Table 2-2. HTMLMediaElement Properties

Property	Purpose
audioTracks	A live MultipleTracklist object representing the audio tracks available in the media resource.
autoplay	Boolean attribute reflecting status of autoplay.
buffered	A TimeRanges object reflecting the ranges of the media resource that have been buffered.
controller	A MediaController object representing the element's current media controller.
controls	Reflects the controls attribute on the media element.
currentSrc	The absolute URL of the selected media resource (read only).
currentTime	The current playback time in seconds.
defaultMuted	The default state of the muted attribute—changing the attribute has no impact on the media element.
defaultPlaybackRate	The desired speed at which the resource is set to play. Not supported by Ogg. A value of 1.0 is normal speed, more is faster, less is slower. A value of 0.0 results in an error. This property is meaningful only if the user agent exposes a user interface allowing the user to set the playback rate.
duration	The length of time of the media, in seconds, or zero if no media is available. If there is media but the length can't be determined the value is NaN; if no predefined length, the value is Inf.
ended	Indicates if media element has ended playing.
error	The MediaError object with information about last error; null if no error.

Property	Purpose
initialTime	The initial playback position, in seconds. Typically a value of 0 (zero).
loop	Reflects the state of the loop boolean attribute.
mediaGroup	Reflects the value of the mediagroup attribute.
muted	A value of true if the media element is muted, or false if not.
networkState	Reflects the current network state for the media element.
paused	Represents whether the media element is paused or not.
playbackRate	The effective playback rate, assuming there is no media controller overriding it.
played	A TimeRanges object that reflects the time ranges the user agent has rendered.
preload	Reflects the contents of the preload attribute.
readyState	Represents the current ready state of the element.
seekable	A TimeRanges object reflecting ranges in the media element the user agent is able to seek to.
seeking	Set to true if user agent is currently seeking a new position in media; false otherwise.
src	Reflects the src attribute of the media element.
startOffsetTime	A Date object representing the current timeline offset.
textTracks	A fixed array of TextTrack objects representing text tracks of media resource.
videoTracks	A live ExclusiveTrackList object representing the video tracks available in the media resource.
volume	The playback volume, in a range of 0.0 (silent) to 1.0 (loudest).

To add a custom control to a media element, you'll need to add HTML that will take the place of the controls. In the example, I want to provide three options to the user: the ability to play, pause, or completely stop the video. I'm using the button elements for all three options, as it is the semantically proper element for the actions.

Both the stop and pause buttons are disabled, by default, since the page loads with the video not playing. In addition, I've added an id attribute to the video element.

The newly adjusted HTML5 page content is shown in Example 2-7. Note that the video element still has the controls attribute. If the user has turned off JavaScript, we still want them to be able to play the video.

Example 2-7. Adjusted HTML5 page, preparing to add a custom media control

```
<!DOCTYPE html>
<head>
   <title>Custom Video Controls</title>
   <meta charset="utf-8" />
</head>
<body>
   <video id="videoobj" width="480" height="270" poster="bigbuckposter.jpg"
      controls>
      <source src="videofile.mp4" type="video/mp4"/>
```

```
        <source src="videofile.webm" type="video/webm" />
    </video>
    <div id="feedback"></div>
    <div id="controls">
        <button id="start">Play</button>
        <button id="stop" disabled>Stop</button>
        <button id="pause" disabled>Pause</button>
    </div>
</body>
```

 As noted in Chapter 1, Opera displays the visual control if scripting is disabled regardless of whether the `controls` attribute is present or not. However, other browsers don't, and this behavior may change in the future. Don't depend on it.

Next, you'll need to add the CSS and JavaScript. The CSS is simple: just turn off the display for the custom controls. When the script is loaded, it tests to see if the user agent can play the video. If so, then the custom control is displayed. If not, then the custom controls remain hidden:

```
<style>
    #controls
        {
        display: none;
        }
</style>
```

Add JavaScript to create an event listener function for each of the new button elements. You could do this in the `window.onload` event handler function, to ensure the buttons have been created and added to the DOM by the time you need to access them. However, since you're also making the controls visible, you may want to add a scripting block following the video/control combination.

The reason for adding a script block to set up the video controls just after the video element is that a video resource can slow the window loading event enough that hiding the default control and displaying the custom control can be distractingly visible to the user. If you don't want to add a scripting block into the web page body, you should use the document's `DOMContentLoaded` event handler instead of `window.onload`. The document's `DOMContentLoaded` event is fired when the DOM is ready, but before external resources—such as video files and images—are loaded. In the examples in this chapter, I use the `DOMContentLoaded` event to trigger a function, `setupControl`, and then keep all of the script within the head element.

 You can also code the function right in the `DOMContentLoaded` `addEventListener` call, rather than define it separately. Since I refer to the function by name several times in the chapter, I've defined it separately.

In the `setupControl` function, you'll also want to add code that tests whether the user agent supports the video object's `canPlayType` property. If it can, the new control is displayed, and the `controls` attribute on the video element is removed. Since it makes no sense to add the button event handler functions if the buttons aren't displayed, the code to set these is also contained within this conditional block:

```
document.addEventListener("DOMContentLoaded", setupControl, false);

function setupControl() {

    // video fallback
    var bbVideo = document.getElementById("videoobj");
    if (bbVideo.canPlayType) {

        // remove default controls
        bbVideo.removeAttribute("controls");

        // display custom controls
        document.getElementById("controls").style.display="block";

        // events for buttons
        document.getElementById("start").
            addEventListener("click",startPlayback,false);
        document.getElementById("stop").
            addEventListener("click",stopPlayback,false);
        document.getElementById("pause").
            addEventListener("click",pausePlayback,false);
    }
```

Before adding the event handler functions for the three buttons, there's one other behavior we have to account for with our custom control: the ability of the user to play and pause the video via the right mouse button context menu.

In the HTML5 specification, *implementors* such as browsers are encouraged to provide media control functionality in the right mouse button context menu for the media element. Not all browsers provide this functionality, but most do (Safari is the only one that doesn't). This functionality is provided regardless of whether the `controls` attribute is present or not. The unintended consequence of providing this functionality means that the user can either use our buttons to control the video playback, the right mouse context menu controls, or both.

The application disables and enables buttons based on the playback state of the video. To ensure the buttons are managed correctly, we'll need to provide event handler functions for the video's `play` and `pause` events:

```
        // disable/enable buttons based on play/pause events
        bbVideo.addEventListener("play",function() {
            document.getElementById("start").disabled=true;
            document.getElementById("pause").disabled=false;
            document.getElementById("stop").disabled=false;
            }, false);

        bbVideo.addEventListener("pause", function() {
```

```
document.getElementById("start").disabled=false;
document.getElementById("pause").disabled=true;
    }, false);
```

When the video is played (regardless of what triggered the play event), the stop and
pause buttons are displayed. When the video playback is paused, the play button is
enabled, and the pause button is disabled. There is no video stop event, so handling
the buttons for the stop request is managed within the stop button's click event handler. It, and the code for the other button click event handlers are added to the script
block next.

The code in each button click event handler function is very simple: it accesses the
video object, and then invokes the video object's play or pause method, depending on
which button was pressed. In addition, if the stop button is clicked, the video object's
currentTime property is also set to 0 (zero). The reason why is that there's no stop
method in the media elements. To stop, you pause the playback, and then reset the
current time. Example 2-8 has the complete scripting block.

Example 2-8. Script block for setting up and operation the custom media controls

```
<script>

    document.addEventListener("DOMContentLoaded", setupControl, false);

    function setupControl() {

        // video fallback
        var bbVideo = document.getElementById("videoobj");
        if (bbVideo.canPlayType) {

            // remove default controls
            bbVideo.removeAttribute("controls");

            // display custom controls
            document.getElementById("controls").style.display="block";

            // events for buttons
            document.getElementById("start").
                addEventListener("click",startPlayback,false);
            document.getElementById("stop").
                addEventListener("click",stopPlayback,false);
            document.getElementById("pause").
                addEventListener("click",pausePlayback,false);

            // disable/enable buttons based on play/pause events
            bbVideo.addEventListener("play",function() {
                document.getElementById("start").disabled=true;
                document.getElementById("pause").disabled=false;
                document.getElementById("stop").disabled=false;
                }, false);

            bbVideo.addEventListener("pause", function() {
                document.getElementById("start").disabled=false;
```

```
            document.getElementById("pause").disabled=true;
        }, false);

    }
}
// start video
function startPlayback() {
    document.getElementById("videoobj").play();
}

// pause video
function pausePlayback() {
    document.getElementById("videoobj").pause();
}

// stop video, return to zero time
// enable play, disable pause and stop
function stopPlayback() {
    var bbVideo = document.getElementById("videoobj");
    bbVideo.pause();
    bbVideo.currentTime=0;
    document.getElementById("start").disabled=false;
    document.getElementById("pause").disabled=true;
    this.disabled=true;
}
</script>
```

Figure 2-5 shows the web page with the customized control opened in IE9. We can now add an overlay to the element, and still manage to control the playback. The controls are plain but they do work, which is what's important. In the next section, we'll get fancier and add additional functionality and a few CSS flourishes.

Figure 2-5. The video element with custom media controls in IE9

Many libraries that provide custom controls have only a play button
that is clicked to play or pause the video. The advantage of this simplified
controls is we don't have to worry about all the disabling and enabling
of buttons.

One other change we could add to the application is to check whether the video can
be successfully played the entire way through before enabling the play button. The
HTMLMediaElement has a property, readyState, that can be tested to see if it has a
value of HAVE_ENOUGH_DATA (numerical value of 4), which indicates a sufficient amount
of data has been loaded so that playback should not trigger a video buffering during
playback. Other available states are:

HAVE_NOTHING (0)
No information and no data is available

HAVE_METADATA (1) and HAVE_CURRENT_DATA(2)
Metadata is available, and data for the immediate playback position is available—
but not enough data to be playable all the way through

HAVE_FUTURE_DATA(3)
Data for playback position is available, and enough data to advance the playback,
but not enough to play all the way through

```
HAVE_ENOUGH_DATA(4)
```
There is enough data to play the video all the way through

There are also events, such as `loadeddata`, that fire when the video is ready to play. However, this event did not fire properly when testing with the target browsers, so I didn't enable its use in the applications in this chapter.

 The HTMLMediaElement is in a great deal of flux at the time this was written. You'll need to check the most recent HTML5 document to verify whether the properties, methods, and events listed in this chapter have changed since this book was written.

Adding CSS and Tracking Playback

The default controls for the media elements provide playback progress. This is rather an important feedback item for media elements, as without it, the web page reader doesn't have a way of estimating how much longer the media resource will play. We want to add the same type of feedback for the custom control.

The obvious semantic choice for tracking progress is the new HTML5 `progress` element. For user agents that implement the control, people will see a visual element in the given operating system's preferred style. People using a browser that hasn't implemented the `progress` element yet will see a text description of how long (in seconds) the media has played.

To add the progress functionality, add the progress element to the HTML, just after the video element, and before the buttons:

```
<video id="videoobj" width="480" height="270" poster="bigbuckposter.jpg"
   controls>
   <source src="videofile.mp4" type="video/mp4"/>
   <source src="videofile.webm" type="video/webm" />
</video>
<div id="feedback">
   <progress id="progressBar" value=0>
      <span id="prog"></span>
   </progress>
</div>
<div id="controls">
   <button id="start">Play</button>
   <button id="stop" disabled>Stop</button>
   <button id="pause" disabled>Pause</button>
</div>
```

We'll also need to incorporate functionality for the `progress` element in the JavaScript. In the previously created `setupControl` function, we'll need to capture an event (`time update`) on the video element and assign a function (`reportProgress`) to the event handler:

```
// setup for video playback
var video = document.getElementById("videoobj");
```

```
document.getElementById("videoobj").
                    addEventListener("timeupdate",reportProgress,false);
```

There are several standard events applicable to the video element, such as the click and onmouseover events. However, there are also media element-specific events, such as timeupdate, and the previously captured play and pause events. I've listed all the media element events in Table 2-3.

Table 2-3. HTMLMediaElement-specific events

Event	Description
abort	If user agent stops media resource fetching, but not because of an error.
canplay	The user agent can resume playing, but enough of the media resource hasn't been downloaded to ensure rendering of entire resource.
canplaythrough	The user agent has fetched enough of the media resource that it can play through all the way to the end.
durationchange	The duration attribute has been changed.
emptied	The media element has become empty, for instance if the media resource was loaded, and the load method is called again.
ended	Signals completion of playback.
error	Signals that an error has occurred.
loadeddata	Signals that the first frame of the media has been loaded.
loadedmetadata	Signals that the metadata has been loaded.
loadstart	The user agent begins looking for the media data, as part of the loading algorithm.
pause	The playback has been paused.
play	The playback is no longer paused and is playing.
playing	Playback can now start after having been paused, or delayed because of lack of media data.
progress	Periodic update of progress of media fetching.
ratechange	The defaultPlaybackRate or playbackRate attributes have been changed.
seeked	Signals end of a seek operation.
seeking	Signals start of a seek operation.
stalled	Triggered when the user agent tries to fetch media data, but for some reason, isn't receiving any data.
suspend	The user agent has suspended fetching media data before finishing.
timeupdate	Signals a change in the current playback position.
volumechange	Triggered when the volume is changed.
waiting	Playback has stopped because the next frame is not available, but the user agent expects it to become available.

In addition to capturing the timeupdate event and assigning an event handler function, we'll need to set the progress element's max attribute to the length of the media resource in order to ensure the progress is measured correctly. We could hardcode the length of the video directly in the attribute, but in this example, we'll access the length of the video using the media element's duration property.

The code to grab the new HTMLMediaElement event and set the progress element's max value, as well as display the progress element, is included in the same code block that previously displayed the custom control and removed the controls attribute. The conditional block now looks like the script shown in Example 2-9.

Example 2-9. The document's DOMContentLoaded setupControl function setting up a page for custom control

```
// setup for video playback
var bbVideo = document.getElementById("videoobj");
if (bbVideo.canPlayType) {

    // remove default controls
    bbVideo.removeAttribute("controls");

    // display custom control and feedback bar
    document.getElementById("controls").style.display="block";
    document.getElementById("feedback").style.display="block";

    // add timeupdate event handler
    bbVideo.addEventListener("timeupdate",reportProgress,false);

    // set max value of  progress
    var progressObj = document.getElementById("progressBar");
    if (progressObj && progressObj.value == 0) {
        document.getElementById("feedback").style.display="block";
        progressObj.max=parseInt(bbVideo.duration);
    }
    // set buttons based on playback
    bbVideo.addEventListener("play",function() {
        document.getElementById("start").disabled=true;
        document.getElementById("pause").disabled=false;
        document.getElementById("stop").disabled=false;
        }, false);

    bbVideo.addEventListener("pause", function() {
        document.getElementById("start").disabled=false;
        document.getElementById("pause").disabled=true;
        }, false);

    // events for buttons
    document.getElementById("start").
        addEventListener("click",startPlayback,false);
    document.getElementById("stop").
        addEventListener("click",stopPlayback,false);
    document.getElementById("pause").
        addEventListener("click",pausePlayback,false);
    }
}
```

The extended test for the progress element (highlighted) is necessary for the code to work in Safari/Webkit Nightly and Firefox 5, since neither supports the progress element, but behave differently towards the element in JavaScript. Safari/Webkit Nightly throws an error if you attempt to access the value attribute on the progress element. Firefox 5 doesn't support the progress element either, but it doesn't return a false value if you just test for the existence of the element. You first need to test for the progress object and then the value property, to get a proper response from both Firefox 5 and Safari 5 (not to mention all the other browsers and their assorted versions and version quirks).

Next we need to code the new event handler function. This function accesses the currentTime attribute to get the current playback position, and uses the value to update the progress element:

```
// update progress
function reportProgress() {

  // set progress element's value
  var time = Math.round(this.currentTime);
  var progressObj = document.getElementById("progressBar");
  if (progressObj && progressObj.max) {
    progressObj.value = time;
  } else {
  // provide text fallback
    document.getElementById("prog").textContent=time + " seconds";
  }
}
```

Since not every user agent that supports the video element also supports the progress element, the progress tracking function also provides a text fallback for that element. The text doesn't show if the progress element is supported.

Lastly, when the reader stops the video, they'll assume that the progress meter will be reset to zero. We'll need to add this code to the stopPlayback event handler function:

```
// stop video, return to zero time
// enable play, disable pause and stop
function stopPlayback() {

  // reset progress bar
  var progressObj = document.getElementById("progressBar");
  if (progressObj && progressObj.max){
    progressObj.value=0;
  }

  var bbVideo = document.getElementById("videoobj");
  bbVideo.pause();
  bbVideo.currentTime=0;
  document.getElementById("start").disabled=false;
  document.getElementById("pause").disabled=true;
  this.disabled=true;
}
```

To finish version two of our custom control, we'll add a little CSS style to our video element and its new custom controls. The video element is styled using the same style-sheet setting shown in Example 2-2. Since the custom controls can now be individually styled, we'll add the same style setting for them as we did for the video element—rounded corner, linear-gradient background, and subtle box shadow:

```css
#start, #stop, #pause
    {
    border: 1px solid #ccc;
    padding: 5px;
    border-radius: 10px;
    }

/* gradients and color backgrounds */
#videoobj, #start, #stop, #pause
    {
    /* add regular background */
    background-color: #ffcccc;

    /* add gradient background */
    background-image: linear-gradient(top, #fff, #fcc);
    background-image: -moz-linear-gradient(top, #fff, #fcc);
    background-image: -webkit-linear-gradient(top, #fff, #fcc);
    background-image: -o-linear-gradient(top, #fff, #fcc);
    background-image: -ms-linear-gradient(top, #fff, #fcc);
    }
/* shadows */
#videoobj, #start, #stop, #pause

    {
    -webkit-box-shadow: 0 0 10px #ccc;
    box-shadow: 0 0 10px #ccc;
    }
```

Lastly, we'll provide the proper spacing for the controls and progress element containers, including turning their display off by default:

```css
#feedback
    {
    display: none;
    margin: 10px 30px;
    }

#controls
    {
    display: none;
    margin: 5px 30px;
    }
```

Figure 2-6 shows the newly designed and styled video element and custom controls, playing in Chrome. The progress element also displays in Opera and Firefox 6 and up. Note the progress showing in the progress element. If we load the page in Firefox 5 and Safari 5, as well as the current Webkit Nightly (at the time this was written) and IE9/10, we'd see text instead.

Figure 2-6. HTML5 video custom control, now with style and progress

Even when the **progress** element works, its appearance is disappointing. At this time, we can't really style it. Something simple, such as setting a new width of the element, causes it to break in Firefox 6. We certainly can't change the fill control.

 The browser companies are experimenting with vendor-specific pseudo-elements that allow application builders to use CSS to style both the progress element and the HTML5 media element controls. However, this work is so new, and varies so much among the organizations that we shouldn't expect to have consistent and standard access to this functionality in the near future.

In addition, the default control for a media element provides feedback on the media resource loading, as well as the playback. We'd have to add two **progress** elements if we want to do the same for our custom control. Either that, or create a custom progress bar, too.

Creating a Custom Progress Bar

Before the **progress** element was defined in HTML5, web application developers used a couple of different scripting tricks in order to create the effect of a bar gradually filling up as a task completes. One I've used successfully in the past is two div elements, one nested in the other and with zero width. As the task progresses, the code changes the width of the inner element. It's a simple, uncomplicated approach. You can even use an animated background to create an animated effect, if you wish.

Since we have enough movement with the video, I decided to forgo the animated background in favor of the linear gradient—gray for the outer div element, and a green reflecting a dominant green from the video for the progressing bar.

The custom progress bar won't be tracking the playback of the video. It's tracking the progress of the video load instead. To track the actual playback, I added another div element, but this time one that has a background character—a purple butterfly like the one that appears throughout the Big Buck Bunny video I used for the examples in this chapter. The HTML for the page, without CSS and without scripting, now looks like the markup in Example 2-10, with the new elements in bold text.

Example 2-10. New web page with custom control and progress bar

```
<!DOCTYPE html>
<head>
    <title>Big Buck Bunny with Custom Controls</title>
    <meta charset="utf-8" />
</head>
<body>
    <div id="container">
        <video id="videoobj" width="480" height="270"
                preload="none" poster="bigbuckposter.jpg" controls>
            <source src="videofile.mp4" type="video/mp4"/>
            <source src="videofile.webm" type="video/webm" />
        </video>
        <div id="controls">
            <button id="start">Play</button>
            <button id="stop" disabled>Stop</button>
            <button id="pause" disabled>Pause</button>
        </div>
        <div id="progressbar">
            <div id="loadingprogress"></div>
            <div id="butterfly"></div>
        </div>
    </div>
</body>
```

In addition, we're going to add a little fun effect for when the video plays. We'll be "turning down the lights in the house" by setting the background color of the page to a darker color while the video is playing, and "turning up the lights in the house" by setting the background back to white when the video is stopped or finished playing. For this effect, we'll need to add a CSS transition for the body element that is specific to only the background color.

We'll keep the button style and button control area style, but remove the feedback styling, as it is no longer needed. Example 2-11 shows the complete stylesheet setting for the newest version of the control.

Example 2-11. Stylesheet settings for custom controls and progress bar

```
video
    {
    /* basic border */
    border: 1px solid #ccc;
    padding: 20px;
    margin: 10px;
    border-radius: 20px;
    }

 /* gradients and color backgrounds */
video, #start, #stop, #pause
    {
    /* add regular background */
    background-color: #ffcccc;

    /* add gradient background */
    background-image: linear-gradient(top, #fff, #fcc);
    background-image: -moz-linear-gradient(top, #fff, #fcc);
    background-image: -webkit-linear-gradient(top, #fff, #fcc);
    background-image: -o-linear-gradient(top, #fff, #fcc);
    background-image: -ms-linear-gradient(top, #fff, #fcc);
    }
/* shadows */
video, #start, #stop, #pause
    {

    -webkit-box-shadow: 0 0 10px #ccc;
    box-shadow: 0 0 10px #ccc;
    }

#controls
    {
    margin: 5px 30px;
    }

#start, #stop, #pause
    {
    border: 1px solid #ccc;
    padding: 5px;
    border-radius: 10px;
    }

body
    {
    /* set up transition */
    -webkit-transition: background-color 1s ease-in-out;
    -moz-transition: background-color 1s ease-in-out;
    -o-transition: background-color 1s ease-in-out;
    -ms-transition: background-color 1s ease-in-out;
```

```css
    transition: background-color 1s ease-in-out;

    background-color: #fff;
    }

#butterfly
    {
    position: absolute;
    left: 0;
    top: -6px;
    background-image: url(butterfly.png);
    width: 30px;
    height: 31px;
    }


 #progressbar
    {
    /* progress bar width and height */
    width: 500px;
    height: 20px;

    /* position and border */
    position: relative;
    border: 1px solid #ccc;
    margin: 10px;
    border-radius: 20px;

    /* add regular background */
    background-color: #cccccc;


    /* add gradient background */
    background-image: linear-gradient(top, #fff, #ccc);
    background-image: -moz-linear-gradient(top, #fff, #ccc);
    background-image: -webkit-linear-gradient(top, #fff, #fcc);
    background-image: -o-linear-gradient(top, #fff, #ccc);
    background-image: -ms-linear-gradient(top, #fff, #ccc);

    /* box shadow */
    -webkit-box-shadow: 0 0 10px #ccc;
    box-shadow: 0 0 10px #ccc;
    }

#loadingprogress
    {
    /* border */
    border-radius: 20px;

    /* beginning height and width */
    height: 20px;
    width: 0;

    /* background */
    background-color: #9acd32;
```

```
background-image: linear-gradient(top, #ffffff, #9acd32);
background-image: -moz-linear-gradient(top, #ffffff, #9acd32);
background-image: -webkit-linear-gradient(top, #ffffff, #9acd32);
background-image: -o-linear-gradient(top, #ffffff, #9acd32);
background-image: -ms-linear-gradient(top, #ffffff, #9acd32);
}
```

In the script, the setupControl function is little different than the ones we've seen earlier. Since any browser that supports the video element can also support the custom progress element, I no longer have to test for progress element support. The only change to the application is the addition of code to capture two more events on the video element: progress and ended. The progress event is triggered periodically as the media resources is loaded, while the ended event is triggered when the media playback finishes:

```
bbVideo.addEventListener("progress", showProgress, false);
bbVideo.addEventListener("ended", endPlayback, false);
```

The pausePlayback function is identical to what we've have in Example 2-8, but both the startPlayback and stopPlayback functions are modified.

The startPlayback function sets the page background to a darker color to emulate the "house lights down" effect. The stopPlayback function does little more than pause the video and set the video currentTime property to zero. It no longer resets the buttons, as it did in the second version of the custom control application. Instead, it calls another function, endPlayback.

The endPlayback function is the function that resets the buttons, as well as the playback indicator and turns up the house lights. It's triggered by the ended event when the video playback is finished. It's also called directly in the stopPlayback method.

The reason we have to separate the two functions is that the video playback is automatically halted when the playback is finished. In addition, the currentTime value is also automatically reset back to zero—we don't need to reset the value. In fact, resetting currentTime to zero in Firefox after the video is finished triggers the video to start playing again.

However, both events—stopping the video by clicking the Stop button, and the video ending naturally—require the same cleanup with the custom controls. This cleanup is contained in the endPlayback function. Example 2-12 shows the three button functions, as well as the new endPlayback function.

Example 2-12. Custom button controls and clean up function for video ending

```
// start video
function startPlayback() {
   document.getElementsByTagName("body")[0].style.backgroundColor="#664c58";
   document.getElementById("videoobj").play();
}

// pause video
function pausePlayback() {
   document.getElementById("videoobj").pause();
```

```
}

// pause video, reset to currentTime of zero
// call function to clean up
function stopPlayback() {
   // reset video
   var bbVideo = document.getElementById("videoobj");
   bbVideo.pause();
   bbVideo.currentTime=0;
   endPlayback();
}

// pause video, reset to currentTime of zero
// call function to clean up
function stopPlayback() {
   // reset video
   var bbVideo = document.getElementById("videoobj");
   bbVideo.pause();
   bbVideo.currentTime=0;
   endPlayback();
}
```

The showProgress function displays the status of the media resource loading. To find out what percentage of the resource is loaded, the code accesses the buffered property on the video. This property is a TimeRanges object, which has three properties: length, start, and end. The length is the number of time ranges within the media resource, while the start and end properties are collections reflecting the start and end of the time range(s).

The showProgress function assumes there is zero or one time range, and accesses the first buffered.end value if there is one time range. Dividing this end value by the video duration returns the percentage of played video. That, multiplied by the progress element's width, with the result rounded, provides the new progress element's width, as shown in Example 2-13.

Example 2-13. Function to track video loading progress

```
// display progress of movie loading
function showProgress() {
   var barwidth = 500;

   // find percentage of video played
   var end = 0;
   if (this.buffered.length >= 1)
      end = this.buffered.end(0);
   var pct = end / this.duration;

   // reset progress width
   var width = Math.round(barwidth * pct);
   document.getElementById("loadingprogress").style.width=width + "px";
}
```

The last function is the `reportProgress` function that moves a slider along the progress indicator to represent the video playback. Instead of setting the video object's `current Time` property to zero, as we have in earlier examples, this time we're accessing its current value with each `progress` event firing. Dividing the current time by the video's duration provides the percentage the video has completed. Multiplying this result by the length of the progress element gives us the position for the indicator. Since the indicator graphic is more than tick mark size, its last few positions are adjusted to ensure it doesn't go too far beyond the end of the progress element, as shown in Example 2-14.

Example 2-14. Function to track the progress of the playback

```
// reset film play marker
function reportProgress() {
    var barwidth = 500;
    var sliderwidth = 30;

    // pct of playback * width
    var time = Math.round(this.currentTime);
    var duration = parseInt(this.duration);
    var position = barwidth * (time / duration);
    if (isNaN(position)) return;

    // position butterfly
    var butterfly = document.getElementById("butterfly");
    if (position <= (barwidth - Math.round(sliderwidth / 2))) {
        butterfly.style.left=position + "px";
    } else {
        butterfly.style.left=barwidth - Math.round(sliderwidth / 2);
    }
}
```

When the web page reader plays the video, the custom progress bar reflects the percentage of video loaded, while the butterfly reflects the current playback. Figure 2-7 shows the application running in IE10, with the video partially loaded and partially played.

Both the progress bar and playback indicator work in all browsers except Opera 11.5. The indicator works with Opera, but at the time this was written, Opera had not yet implemented the `buffered` property in the released version of Opera. The `buffered` property is supported, however, in Opera.next (Opera 12). In addition, Chrome won't trigger the `progress` event on the video if it already has the video cached. When you click the pause or stop button, it does fire the `progress` event once, and the bar is updated to show that the file is 100% cached. However, it doesn't fire the `progress` event when you click play. To test the progress bar in Chrome, you'll need to clear your cache first.

Figure 2-7. Playing the third version of the custom controls application in IE10

There's just one other functionality that we have with the default controls that we don't have with the custom controls: being able to jump to different parts of the film during playback. We'll add this functionality with version four of the custom control, discussed in the next section.

The Custom Control and Seekability

The ability to move through a media resource file during playback is known as *seeking*. From earlier tables reflecting the HTMLMediaElement properties and events, we know there is one property, `seeking`, which is set to *true* when the video player is seeking a new playback position. Another property, `seekable`, returns a `TimeRanges` object with the time ranges the user agent can seek to. Seeking also triggers an event, `seeking`, when it is performing the seek operation, and `seeked`, when the operation is finished.

All of this is dependent on one thing, though: something triggering the seek operation. Version four of the custom controls will provide this functionality by allowing the web page reader to indicate on the progress bar where they want the playback to continue.

Providing the ability for the reader to click anywhere on the progress bar in order to change where the playback occurs begins with adding a new event handler, this time for the click event on the progress bar. The code is added to the document's setupControl function:

```
// progress bar event
var prog = document.getElementById("progressbar");
prog.addEventListener("click",seekPlayback, false);
```

The new function, seekPlayback, accesses the event element in order to access the position of the click within the progress bar. The code then uses this value to calculate the playback location, as shown in Example 2-15.

Example 2-15. Providing the seek functionality

```
// seekPlayback
function seekPlayback(e) {
    var barwidth = 500;

    // find click position
    var x = e.pageX - this.offsetLeft;

    // translate to video position
    var pct = x / barwidth;
    var bbVideo = document.getElementById("videoobj");

    // now position playback
    var newPos = Math.round(bbVideo.duration * pct);
    bbVideo.currentTime = newPos;
}
```

Notice that we don't have to reset the indicator at the same time we change the playback position. That's because changing the playback position doesn't stop the video playing, and the playing still triggers the timeupdate event. The next time the timeupdate event fires, the indicator is moved to the new position.

The only other change necessary is in the showProgress function, covered in Example 2-13. Previously, the code made an assumption that there was only one time range. However, the seek operation has changed this and we now have to deal with a possible set of time ranges.

Since we're not dealing with one time range, we'll have to calculate the progress percentage by subtracting each time range's start value from the end value, and then sum the results. Other than this change, though, the rest of the function remains the same, as shown in Example 2-16.

Example 2-16. Modified progress function accounting for multiple time ranges

```
// display progress of movie loading
function showProgress() {
    var barwidth = 500;
    var bbVideo = document.getElementById("videoobj");
```

```
// since there's now the possibility of multiple time ranges
var end = 0;
for (var i = 0; i < bbVideo.buffered.length; i++) {
  end += (bbVideo.buffered.end(i) - bbVideo.buffered.start(i));
}

// find percentage of playback to duration
var pct = end / bbVideo.duration;
var bar = document.getElementById("loadingprogress");

// adjust the progress
var width = (barwidth * pct);
document.getElementById("loadingprogress").style.width=width + "px";
}
```

Now when you play the video file, you can click around the progress bar and cause the playback to change to the new position. Since this functionality is still *very* new, browser behavior does vary:

- Opera allows you to easily and quickly change the playback position, and starting with Opera 12, also supports the buffered property, so the progress bar works with this newest browser version.
- Firefox 5 and up supports both the ability to change playback position, and the progress bar.
- Safari 5 (and Webkit Nightly) allows us to click on the progress bar, but only within the areas where the video has already been loaded (the portion of the progress bar already filled in). This is the same behavior as the default control.
- Chrome 12 lets us change the playback position, but has problems with showing the progress. The Chrome Canary build does a little better job with showing progress, but still seems to have issues with the functionality. Looking more closely at the browser's behavior, it doesn't appear that Chrome supports groups of time ranges within buffered yet.
- Both IE9 and IE10 support the ability to change playback position, and the progress bar. However, when you seek beyond the currently buffered video time range, the progress bar resets back to zero. Examining the results more closely shows us that Microsoft is maintaining only one time range at a time.

If you want a more up close and personal look at how the time ranges work, add an empty div element with an id of *test* to the end of the HTML for the document. Then change the buffered array processing to the following:

```
for (var i = 0; i < this.buffered.length; i++) {
  document.getElementById("test").innerHTML = i + " " +
            this.buffered.start(i) + " " + this.buffered.end(i);
  end += (this.buffered.end(i) - this.buffered.start(i));
}
```

Figure 2-8 shows the video playing in Firefox, after a couple of new positions are picked for playback, and with the time range feedback code. The time range information is below the controls, to the left of the page. It's rather interesting to see the number of time ranges increase and then decrease, as the ranges are seemingly buffered and then merged with other buffered ranges.

Figure 2-8. Trying out version four of the custom control, with seekability

Other options you can add are support for a volume control and *fullscreen mode*. Volume control is simple: add a range input element or other slider-like control to adjust the volume using the HTMLMediaElement's `volume` property—from 0 (silent) to 1 (loudest).

Unfortunately, there is no simple support for fullscreen mode. It isn't part of any of the HTML5 media element interfaces, nor is it supported in most browsers. Webkit does offer a vendor-specific method, `webkitEnterFullscreen`:

```
videoobj.webkitEnterFullscreen();
```

This method currently only works in Safari 5 and the Webkit Nightly. When the video is in fullscreen mode, the default fullscreen video control is displayed, regardless of whether the video element's `controls` attribute is present or not.

Other browsers don't provide anything so simple to use. What you have to do is get window measurements and resize the video to go fullscreen, making sure to store previous video element measurements for when the person exits fullscreen mode. You can get a feel for the amount of work involved by looking through the JavaScript libraries that provide custom controls, covered in Chapter 3 and in the appendix. It is not a complicated process, but the amount of code necessary does make it a tedious process.

Other than a volume control and support for fullscreen access, our custom control has most of the functionality of the built-in control, but with the added benefit being able to customize both the appearance and behavior of the control.

Debugging and Discovering Browser Support

In the next couple of chapters, I'm going to cover some of the more advanced features for the HTML5 media elements. Before I do, though, I wanted to demonstrate a technique you can use to determine what each browser does or doesn't support on the media elements. This technique also demonstrates how you can debug your media applications in your favorite browser.

All browsers either have a built-in debugger, or have one that you can install. These debuggers each have a way of exposing the properties, methods, and events supported on an HTML element. All you need to do is obtain a reference to the media object instance.

To explore what's available for audio and video elements, add a video and audio element to a web page, and then add a simple JavaScript object that gets a reference to both, as shown in Example 2-17.

Example 2-17. A simple method for exploring a browser's implementation of the video and audio elements

```
<!DOCTYPE html>
<head>
<title>Exploring the elements</title>
<meta charset="utf-8" />
   <script>
      window.onload=function() {
         var videoobj = document.getElementById("videoobj");
         var audioobj = document.getElementById("audioobj");
         var test = 0;
      }
   </script>
</head>
<body>
   <video id="videoobj" controls>
      <source src="videofile.mp4" type="video/mp4" />
      <source src="videofile.webm" type="video/webm" />
      <track label="English subtitles" kind="subtitles" srclang="en"
          src="subtitles.vtt" default />
   </video>
   <audio id="audioobj" controls>
      <source src="audiofile.mp3" type="audio/mp3" />
      <source src="audiofile.ogg" type="audio/ogg" />
```

```
    </audio>
</body>
```

Open the page in a browser that supports a debugger, or has a debugger installed, and then start the debugger. Set a break point on the following line of script:

```
var test = 0;
```

When the script is run and reaches this break point, the debugger has references to both the audio and video objects, and you can explore their implementations within the debugger.

Figure 2-9 shows the video element in the newest Canary build for Google's Chrome. Notice the support for several new vendor-specific properties (designated by the "webkit" prefix). Notice also the support for the seekable property, which is of type *TimeRanges*. This property is formally supported in the HTML5 specification, and, in fact, was necessary in order to implement the fourth version of the custom media control, described in the last section.

To access the debugger for our five target browsers, follow these guidelines:

- For Chrome, access the Tools main menu (look for the wrench), then the Tools submenu, and finally select Developer Tools.

- For Opera, access the Tools main menu, then the Advanced submenu option, and select Opera Dragonfly.

- For Safari/Webkit Nightly, select the Page main menu (document icon), and then the Develop submenu option. From the options that appear, select Start Debugging JavaScript.

- For Internet Explorer, press F12, or select the Tools main menu option, then the F12 Developer Tools submenu option. The Developer Tools open in a separate window. You'll need to enable script debugging. For IE10, select the Debug menu option, then F12 Developer Tools.

- For Firefox, you'll need to install Firebug. Once installed, make sure the Add-on Bar is showing, and then click the Firebug icon in the Add-on Bar.

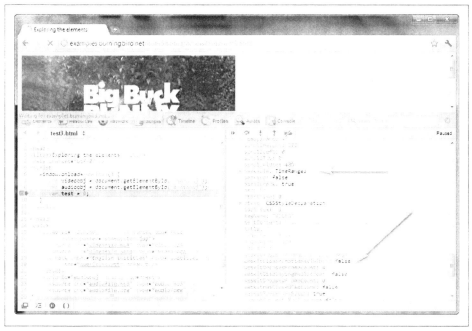

Figure 2-9. Demonstrating how to view the application interface for the video element in Chrome (Canary Build)

For all the browsers, you may need to specifically enable script debugging the first time you access the debugger. Check with the browser documentation to find out the details.

All browser debuggers support the same technique to set a break point: you click to the left of the line number of the code line where you want program execution to pause. When you reload the page or restart the script (whatever you need to do to trigger the break point in the debugger), the code execution halts at this break point.

Another universal: explore the local variables in a box to the right of the debugger. In this case, the local variables we're interested in are audioobj and videoobj. The reason for the third line of code in the script block is so that we have a break point we can reach *after* these objects have been created.

Firebug, Dragonfly, and the Chrome and Safari debuggers display a list of local variables in a single pane with other variables, but should be immediately apparent. With Dragonfly, they're in a panel labeled *inspection*; for Chrome and Safari, they're in a panel labeled with *Scope Variables*; in Firebug, clicking the *Watch* tab brings up the local (and global) variables, with the local variables, first. With IE, you'll need to click the *Locals* tab in the right side of the debugger.

Once you've done all this, you can see each browser's HTML5 video and audio element support at a glance, and what the implementation looks like. Figure 2-9 demonstrated this with Chrome. Figure 2-10 demonstrates this using the IE9 debugger.

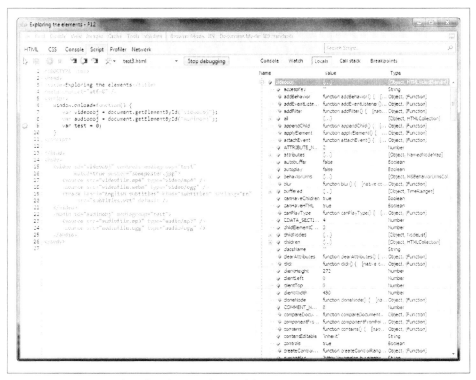

Figure 2-10. Inspecting the video object in the IE9 debugger

Media Elements, Multiple Tracks, and Accessibility

The area most in flux in relation to the new media elements has to do with synchronized media playback, multiple audio, video, and text tracks, and media element accessibility. As to be expected, these areas also have the least implementation support.

A new addition to the HTML5 media elements is the new media controller object. This object provides for synchronized playback among multiple audio and video elements in a web page. When implemented, we should be able to play video and/or audio files in multiple elements in the web page via one controller user interface.

Another new addition is support for multiple audio and video tracks within the media resource. When this functionality is implemented, we should be able to pick from among a list of audio tracks in different languages, play director commentary along with the video, or enjoy picture-in-picture support.

There's also browser support for multiple text tracks, too. Currently, browsers parse the track element and it becomes part of the Document Object Model (DOM), but no browser yet processes the track element's contents and provides the caption or subtitle text. Happily, though, there are JavaScript libraries that can process the captions or subtitles within the track elements, giving us at least some interim functionality, as we'll see at the end of the chapter.

No firm commitment has been made—either in the W3C or by the browser makers—as to what text format to support for text tracks. There are multiple subtitle and caption formats currently in use with video files, such as SubRip (SRT), but none of them provide the additional functionality many believe is needed for web-based media players. There are also parallel, and somewhat competitive, efforts to define what this format is going to be, though there is a possibility user agents will need to support more than one text track format.

So, welcome to the chaotic side of the HTML media elements.

Media Controllers and the MediaController Interface

A new attribute, mediagroup, has been added to the audio and video element specification. This attribute is used to group media elements together so their playback is synchronized. The existence of mediagroup attribute generates an instance of a *media controller* that controls the various media resources' playback..

How would something like a media controller work? One possible use case is a single video with a separate audio resource, as well as a separate sign language video. Only one of the elements, the main video, is created with a controls attribute. Clicking the play button on the video also triggers a play on the other two resources. Clicking on the pause button pauses all three resources:

```
<video poster="some.png" controls mediagroup="altogethernow">
    <source src="videofile.mp4" type="video/mp4" />
    <source src="videofile.ogg" type="video/ogg" />
</video>
<video poster="sign.png" mediagroup="altogethernow">
    <source src="videofilesign.mp4" type="video/mp4" />
    </source src="videofilesign.ogg" type="video/ogg" />
</video>
<audio mediagroup="altogethernow">
    <source src="audiofile.mp3" type="audio/mp3" />
    <source src="audiofile.ogg" type="audio/ogg" />
</audio>
```

Among other use cases is that of creating a picture-in-picture effect by scaling one video and overlaying it on the other, and then adding the controls attribute to the larger, primary video.

There are many possible uses for this type of functionality and, just as with a single resource, you can use JavaScript to control the media controller (and hence the playback of the entire group of media resources).

The MediaController object provides an interface for accessing the media controller in script. It supports two methods:

play
    Sets the paused attribute to false and causes playback to resume on all slaved media resources.

pause
    Sets the paused attribute to true and causes playback to pause on all slaved media resources.

The MediaController methods are similar to the methods for HTMLMediaElement described in Chapter 2. The difference lies in the fact that more than one media resource is controlled by an individual action.

The properties for the MediaController are also very similar to those listed for the HTMLMediaElement in Table 2-2 in Chapter 2, as shown in Table 3-1. Again, the primary difference is that the property's value isn't dependent on the state of one media resource, but a group of media resources. In the HTML5 specification, all of the media resources controlled by a media controller are known as *slaved media resources*.

Table 3-1. Methods for MediaController Interface

Property	Purpose
buffered	Returns a reference to the TimeRanges object, representing the time ranges of the slaved media resources
seekable	Returns a reference to the TimeRanges object, representing the time ranges the user agent can seek to
duration	The difference between earliest playable moment and latest playable moment
currentTime	Current playback time in seconds
paused	Set to true if playback currently paused; otherwise false
played	A TimeRanges object representing a union of the played time ranges in all of the slaved media elements
defaultPlayback Rate	The default rate of playback (can be changed)
playbackRate	Current playback rate
volume	Change volume, from 0.0 to 1.0
muted	Set to true if all audio is muted

MediaController events are also very similar to HTMLMediaElement events, as shown in Table 3-2. They key difference is, again, an event is only triggered when conditions are met for all of the slaved media resources. Take an event like waiting. It's triggered in the HTMLMediaElement when playback is blocked because the next frame isn't currently available, but the user agent is expecting it to become available. With the MediaController, waiting generally means the same thing, but it comes about because one of the media resources is blocked, not necessarily because all the media resources are blocked.

The MediaController adds new meaning to the old phrase: all for one, and one for all.

Table 3-2. MediaController Events

Event	When Invoked
canplay	The user agent can resume playing, but enough of the slaved media resources haven't been downloaded to ensure rendering of resources.
canplaythrough	The user agent has fetched enough of all the slaved media resources that it can play through all the way to the end.
durationchange	The duration attribute has been updated.

Event	When Invoked
emptied	All slaved media finished playback or no longer a slaved media resource.
ended	Playback in all slaved media sources is finished.
loadedmetadata	Signals when metadata in all slaved media resources is loaded.
loadeddata	Signals when data in all slaved media resources is loaded.
pause	When the pause attribute is set to true, and playback has paused.
play	The slaved media resources are no longer paused and are playing
ratechange	Triggered when the playback rate is changed for all slaved media resources.
timeupdate	Signals a change in the current playback position.
volumechange	The volume has changed for all slaved media resources.
waiting	Playback has stopped because the next frame in at least one slaved media source is not available, but the user agent expects it to become available

The MediaController's methods, properties, and events are a subset of those available to HTMLMediaElement. In particular, notice that there are no seeking events, nor events associated with the user agent aborting data loading or being stalled.

The events, as well as the additional properties and methods, should still be available on individual media resources. To access individual values, focus on the media resource you would consider the master resource.

 There is no support for media controllers at the time this was written. Be sure to check the current HTML5 specification for changes to the methods and properties. In addition, check the documentation for your browsers of interest to see what support they have for the interface. You can also use the technique described at the end of Chapter 2 to manually check implementation details for the media elements in your favorite browser.

Multiple Tracks and the Track List Interfaces

Another very new addition to the HTML5 specification related to the media elements is support for a collection of track lists—whether embedded directly in the media resource, added to the resource programmatically, or added using the track element:

```
<video controls poster="poster.jpg" width="480" height="204">
  <source src="videofile.m4v" type="video/mp4" />
  <source src="videofile.webm" type="video/webm" />
  <track label="English subtitles" kind="subtitles"
        srclang="en" src="videofile.vtt" default />
  <track label="Chapter List" kind="chapters"
        srclang="en" src="videofile_chaps.vtt" />
  <track label="Captions" kind="captions"
        srclang="en" src="videofile_caps.vtt" />
</video>
```

Why would your media resource need to have more than one audio or video track? Well, think of your DVDs and Blu-Rays. Many times they provide audio tracks for different languages, as well as tracks for a director voiceover, or even a copy of the movie with embedded audio/visual commentary.

In addition, you may have text tracks for subtitles in various languages, as well as captions, and even a chapter list.

Though we're not re-creating your DVD or Blu-Ray player in a little box in a web page, people have become more sophisticated about what to expect from a movie playback experience. The more of the expected functionality we can provide, the better the experience for those visiting our web pages or using our applications.

 You can add text tracks to the media element declaratively within the HTML, or programmatically using JavaScript, but you can't add additional audio or video tracks. These have to be added using an audio or video editor.

Audio and Video Track Collections

The collection of audio tracks can be accessed from the HTMLMediaElement's `audioTracks` property, while the collection of video tracks can be accessed from the `videoTracks` property.

The `audioTracks` attribute is of type AudioTrackList, while the `videoTracks` property is of type VideoTrackList. The difference between the audio and video collection interfaces is that more than one audio track can play at a time, but only one video track can play at any given time.

 The audio and video track list functionality is so new in the HTML5 specification that it had been completely redesigned between the time I finished this chapter and when the tech editors had finished reviewing it. I expect it to continue to change dramatically after this book is published.

Both AudioTrackList and VideoTrackList support a property, `length`, with the number of tracks for each type, respectively. They both also contain another *readonly* property, `kind`, that contains a reference to the type of track. Table 3-3 contains a listing of the possible category values this property may contain (derived from a table given in the HTML5 specification).

Table 3-3. Video and Audio Category Values

Category	Definition	Applies to...	Example
alternative	A possible alternative to main track	Audio and Video	Ogg: "audio/alternate" or "video/alternate"
description	An audio description of a video track	Audio only	Ogg: "audio/audiodesc"
main	The primary audio or video track	Audio and Video	Ogg: "audio/main" or "video/main"
sign	A sign-language interpretation of an audio track	Video only	Ogg: "video/sign"
translation	A translated version of the main track	Audio only	Ogg: "audio/dub"
"" (empty string)	No explicit kind	Audio and video	Any role not matching given categories

The objects also support *getters* that allow application developers to access specific tracks using an index value:

```
var specTrack = videoObjTracks(1);
```

The developer can also use the getTrackById method (passing in the identifier of the track), if the media resource supports track identifiers. Other properties for both objects are:

label
> Track label if one is provided by the media resource

language
> The BCP 47 language tag (such as *en* for English) for the track

enabled
> Whether the track is enabled or not

Both objects support one event, change, triggered when the track selection has changed. In addition, the VideoTrackList object also supports another property, selected, which is set to true for the track currently selected; false for other tracks.

Web applications can provide functionality to select audio or video tracks, but this information can also be defined within the HTML, using syntax such as the following:

```
<video src="videofile#track=Alternative"></video>
```

This only works if the media resource provides support for the Media Fragments URI, another new specification being developed at the W3C.

 The Media Fragments URI specification can be found at *http://www.w3 .org/TR/media-frags/*. This specification is only in draft state, and may change considerably before reaching recommendation status.

When browsers do provide support for multiple track lists, they'll provide an option in the default user interface to select from among a list of available audio tracks.

How would the multiple audio track support work? If a video has multiple language translations, a menu could be provided allowing the user to pick which language he or she prefers. Users could also be given the option of playing an alternative track, rather than the main track—similar to playing the extended cut versions in our DVDs and Blu-Rays.

Unfortunately, no browser—released, beta, or otherwise—currently supports the HTMLMediaElement audioTracks or videoTracks properties, or the associated interfaces.

Multiple Text Tracks

In addition to support for multiple video and audio tracks, HTML5 also provides support for multiple text tracks, as well. The text tracks are accessed through an array of TextTrack objects via HTMLMediaElement's textTracks property.

The TextTrack interface has no methods but does have several properties:

activeCues
> A live TextTrackCueList object representing the text track list of cues for the Text Track objects that are flagged as active.

cues
> A live TextTrackCueList object representing the text track list of cues. The cues provide information to the user agent for rendering.

kind
> The kind of text track object.

language
> The text track language of the text track.

readyState
> The ready state for the text track.

mode
> Whether the text track is on or off, and whether hidden or not.

The kind and language attributes will be discussed in more detail in the next section, covering the track element. The readyState property can be one of four constant values:

NONE (0)
> The text track is not loaded.

LOADING (1)
> The text track is loading.

LOADED (2)
> The text track is loaded.

ERROR (3)
The text track failed to load.

The `mode` property can be one of three constant values:

OFF (0)
The text track is disabled.

HIDDEN (1)
The text track is hidden.

SHOWING (2)
The text track is showing.

The `TextTrackCueList` object is, itself, made up of `TextTrackCue` objects. Each cue has a property, `track` (which is the track the cue is related to), a unique `id`, and `startTime` and `endTime` properties that reflect the cue's start and end times (in numeric seconds) within the media resource's timeline. There are also methods that can be used to get the cue source, both as text (`getCueAsSource`), and HTML (`getCueAsHTML`). In addition, another property, `pauseOnExit`, reflects whether the `pause-on-exit` flag is set, which indicates whether the playback is to pause when the cue finishes.

Unlike the video and audio tracks, text tracks can be added to the HTMLMediaElement's textTracks array via three means. How they're added also determines how the tracks are sorted.

The order by which the tracks are sorted is:

1. Text tracks via the `track` element, in tree order.
2. Text tracks added using the HTMLMediaElement `addTextTrack` method, mentioned in Table 2-1 in Chapter 2.
3. Text tracks embedded directly in the media resource, in whatever order the media container specifies.

When browsers implement text tracks, they should provide a means in the control UI by which users can select which track is to play.

Supposedly Safari has implemented support for tracks embedded in video files. However, when I tried this with an MP4 video with an embedded captions file in SRT format, Safari couldn't even play the video—much less show the captions. None of the other browsers have implemented support for text tracks at this time.

Happily, though, there is a way of enabling captions, subtitles, and other forms of text tracks right now, using the `track` element and JavaScript.

The Track Element

Though browsers will eventually provide support for embedded text tracks, HTML5 provides an additional technique to add text tracks to a media element: the `track` element. In addition to zero or more `source` elements, the HTML5 `video` and `audio` elements also support zero or more `track` elements.

 For this section, I switched from Big Buck Bunny to Sintel, another video from the Blender open movie project. The reason why is that Sintel has dialog, and the project provides subtitle files in SRT format in several different languages. Access Sintel videos and SRT files at *http://www .sintel.org/*.

A typical use case for a `track` element is the following, where a video file has an associated text track used to provide English captions for the video:

```
<video controls poster="someposter.jpg">
   <source src="videofile.m4v" />
   <source src="videofile.webm" />
   <track label="English subtitles" kind="captions"
          srclang="en" src="trackfile_en.srt" default />
</video>
```

The `track` element's attributes are:

`kind`
> The track category

`src`
> The URL for the track source file

`srclang`
> The track language

`label`
> The label to display for the track file in a menu

`default`
> Used to indicate this track is enabled unless the user signifies a preference for another track; can only be used on one track element

The `kind` and `srclang` attributes are equivalent to the `TextTrack` object's `kind` and `language` properties, discussed in the last section. The `language` attribute takes a BCP 47 language designation, such as *en* for English.

The proper formation of the language tag is far beyond the scope of this book. In the examples, I use *en* for English, since I primarily work with English language materials. For more on the language tag, I recommend an article from the W3C, "Language tags in HTML and XHTML", at *http://www.w3.org/International/articles/language-tags/*.

The kind attribute can be one of the following values:

- subtitles
- captions
- descriptions
- chapters
- metadata

To add a new text track to the media element, just add the track element, providing the information describing the text file. If you add more than one track element, add the default attribute to only one track element.

Are Subtitles and Captions the Same Thing?

Folks speak of subtitles and captions interchangeably, but they aren't the same thing.

A subtitle is a way of providing a textual translation of speech in a video. For instance, many of us have watched various Godzilla movies in Japanese but with English subtitles.

The use of captions, or more properly, *closed captioning*, not only provides a textual description of what's being said, but also a textual description of other sounds that are important for the video watcher to understand what's happening. Text can include cues about a doorbell ringing, a faraway scream of terror, or even off-screen laughter— any additional information that ensures those who can't hear the audio can still appreciate the video.

Track File Formats

There is no preferred format for the track files. An existing format for captions and subtitles embedded in video is the SubRip file format, given a *.srt* extension. Earlier work on providing a standard format for HTML5 media resources was called WebSRT and was based on SRT. However, this effort was eventually renamed to WebVTT (Web Video Text Tracks), and is still loosely based on the SRT format. Work in the WebVTT format is ongoing with the WHATWG (Web Hypertext Application Technology Working Group), though there has been some moves to also start up a W3C working group for the format.

At this time, there is no preferred format. Which you use depends on the tools you use to implement the subtitles and captions.

 There's also interest in the W3C in using the Timed Text Markup Language as a format for the track files. However, this specification is more complicated than WebVTT or SRT because of its dependence on XML, though there has been discussion of creating a JSON version of TTML for use with HTML5 media resources. You can find more on TTML at *http://www.w3.org/TR/ttaf1-dfxp/*, more on the SRT format at *http://www.matroska.org/technical/specs/subtitles/srt.html*, and you can check out the capabilities of the WebVTT format in an author-friendly format at *http://www.delphiki.com/webvtt/*.

SRT

The SRT format is extremely simple. SRT files are text files with a set of lines, each one a specific subtitle. Each subtitle begins with a sequential number, followed by a timeline on a second line, and then the subtitle text on a third line. Subtitles are separated from each other by blank lines. From the Sintel English subtitle file:

```
1
00:01:47,250 --> 00:01:50,500
This blade has a dark past.

2
00:01:51,800 --> 00:01:55,800
It has shed much innocent blood.

3
00:01:58,000 --> 00:02:01,450
You're a fool for traveling alone,
so completely unprepared.

4
00:02:01,750 --> 00:02:04,800
You're lucky your blood's still flowing.
```

This subset of four subtitles from the file demonstrates about all you need to know about SRT. The first line for each subtitle is the unique subtitle number. The second line is the time when the subtitle should appear, and the time when it should disappear. The subtitle is next, and may be on more than one line. The subtitle is then followed by a blank line.

The time format is hh:mm:ss,ms and a double dash (--) and right angle bracket (>) is used to separate the beginning and ending time. Note that the separator between the seconds and milliseconds is a comma (,).

The SRT files can be encoded using ANSI, Unicode Little Endian, UTF-8, and others, but for use in HTML5 video track elements, you should stick with UTF-8. The MIME type is text/plain.

Chances are browsers will end up supporting SRT files because of their popularity. And they'll work, as is. However, one reason why people wanted something different is because web developers want to have more control over how the subtitles are displayed. That's what led to the work in WebVTT, discussed next.

WebVTT

At first glance, WebVTT looks very similar to SRT. Each subtitle begins with a number, followed by a timeline, and then the subtitle. The file extension is *.vtt*, rather than *.srt*. Where WebVTT differs from SRT is in providing several cue settings that can be used to control the subtitles display.

A WebVTT has the following as the first line in the file:

```
WEBVTT
```

What follows is a set of subtitle entries, each proceeded by a number representing their order. The following is the first four subtitles for Sintel, converted from SRT to WebVTT:

```
WEBVTT

1
00:01:47.250 --> 00:01:50.500
This blade has a dark past.

2
00:01:51.800 --> 00:01:55.800
It has shed much innocent blood.

3
00:01:58.000 --> 00:02:01.450
You're a fool for traveling alone,
so completely unprepared.

4
00:02:01.750 --> 00:02:04.800
You're lucky your blood's still flowing.
```

The primary difference between the SRT subtitles shown in the last section and the WebVTT version is in the timeline. The WebVTT timeline uses a period (.) to separate the milliseconds from the seconds, while SRT uses a comma (,). Other than the first line and swapping the commas out, the file works as is, for a WebVTT track file.

Where WebVTT differs significantly from SRT is in the ability to provide cue settings. Table 3-4 shows the different cue settings available for use with WebVTT, and how they work.

The cue settings are positioned to the right of the timeline:

```
00:01:47.250 --> 00:01:50.500 D:vertical
```

Table 3-4. WebVTT cue settings

Setting	Usage
Text direction	
D:vertical	Vertical text (vertical going left)
D:vertical-lr	Vertical text (vertical going left)
Line positioning relative to frame	
L:[number]%	Number is a positive number
L:[number]	Number can be positive or negative
Text positioning	
T:[number]%	Number is a positive number
Text size	
S:[number]%	Number is a positive number
Text alignment	
A:start	At the start
A:middle	In the middle
A:end	At the end

Most of the cue settings are self-explanatory. If you want the text to align at the end and be positioned in the middle of the video frame, use the following:

```
1
00:01:47.250 --> 00:01:50.500 A:end L:50%
This blade has a dark past.
```

The impact of this cue, using one of the JavaScript library that provides interim support for WebVTT, can be seen in Figure 3-1. The text floats to the middle of the frame and is shifted to the right.

In addition to the cue settings, you can also use regular inline markup, such as the following, within the text:

- Bold: the text
- Italic: <i>the text</i>
- Underline: <u>the text</u>
- Ruby annotations: <ruby>the text<rt>annotation</rt></ruby>

Because of the use of markup, you'll need to escape some characters if you want them literally interpreted:

- & is replaced by &
- < is replaced by <
- > is replaced by >

Figure 3-1. Applying a cue setting to a WebVTT subtitle

You can also provide a `class`, and then provide a style setting to change as many properties of the text as you wish. The syntax for the use of `class` is the following, where the open c tag setting provides the class name:

```
<c.someclass>the text</c>
```

Note that the closing tag does not repeat the class name.

Example 3-1 shows the first several subtitle entries in the *sintel.vtt* file with both cue settings and use of HTML markup.

Example 3-1. WebVTT subtitle entries with cue settings and HTML markup

```
WEBVTT

1
00:01:47.250 --> 00:01:50.500 A:end L:50%
This blade has a <i>dark past</i>.

2
00:01:51.800 --> 00:01:55.800
It has shed much innocent <c.blood>blood</c>.

3
00:01:58.000 --> 00:02:01.450 A:start L:10%
You're a <b>fool</b> for traveling alone,
so completely unprepared.
```

```
4
00:02:01.750 --> 00:02:04.800
You're lucky your <c.blood>blood's</c>
still flowing.

5
00:02:05.250 --> 00:02:06.300
<c.grateful>Thank you.</c>
```

 Originally, the first line of an WebVTT file was WEBVTT FILE, but this recently changed to just WEBVTT. Not all JavaScript libraries support WEBVTT by itself and the specification may end up supporting both.

The following is the CSS for the two class names used in the markup. The CSS is included in a regular CSS stylesheet attached to the same page as the video element with the associate WebVTT track:

```
<style>
.grateful
{
   background-color: orange;
   color: black;
}
.blood
{
   color: red;
   font-weight: bold;
}
```

One potential new change for WebVTT under consideration is being able to embed style settings directly in the WebVTT file. These style settings, though, wouldn't be for use with HTML5 web video use, since we can add CSS via the web page. They're more for other applications, such as Quicktime that don't support CSS.

Figure 3-2 shows the video playing in Opera, and the rather lurid use of font color to highlight the word "blood".

A last annotation you can use with WebVTT is the voice cue tag:

```
<v.Shelley>Hey! This is me talking!
```

Currently the specification doesn't provide a closing voice tag, but this is likely to change to the following:

```
<v.Shelley>Hey! This is me talking!</v>
```

You can also support a karaoke-style (step-by-step) presentation, using inline time-stamps for each step:

```
04:18:00.657-->04:19:00.000
One...<04:18:20.000>Two...<04:18:40.000>Three...
```

Figure 3-2. Use of class name and CSS to highlight a specific word in the subtitle

It's all well and good to talk about SRT and WebVTT and how you can use annotation and markup to control the subtitle and caption text, but what good is any of this when browsers haven't implemented track support yet?

Luckily, we don't have to wait for the browsers to finish implementing the HTML5 video and audio elements in order to try out captions and subtitles and all the WebVTT annotations.

 For more on WebVTT, I recommend Julien Villetorte's web page, "Understanding WebVTT file format" at *http://www.delphiki.com/webvtt/*. In addition, the Leanback Player site provides an excellent author view of the WebVTT specification, at *http://leanbackplayer.com/other/webvtt .html*.

JavaScript Support for Subtitles and Captions

The track element provides the URL for the text tracks. Combine this with XMLHttpRequest to access the file, and JavaScript and CSS in order to display the contents, and you now have a way of providing captions and subtitles, without waiting for the browser.

Of course, processing the track files and displaying the result is not a trivial task. You not only have to parse out the subtitle entries, but also apply any annotation if the file is WebVTT. Then you have to provide a way for the user to select whether to display captions or subtitles, and also display them in such a way that they effectively provide subtitle/caption support without overshadowing the video.

All of this is doable, with a lot of time. Happily, though, we don't have to create any of this functionality (well, not unless we want to).

There are various HTML5 video player applications, libraries, and utilities, but I picked three for this chapter because of their subtitle support. The first is Captionator, created by Christopher Giffard. The second is Playr, by Julien Villetorte. The third is the Leanback player, which also provides excellent keyboard access.

 Download Captionator from *https://github.com/cgiffard/Captionator.* Download Playr at *http://www.delphiki.com/html5/playr/.* Access the Leanback Player at *http://dev.mennerich.name/showroom/html5_video/.*

Captionator

Captionator is quite easy to use. You add a link to the JavaScript library to your HTML page, and then a brief block of code to trigger the application when the window is loaded:

```
<script type="text/javascript" src="js/captionator.js"></script>
<script type="text/javascript">
   window.addEventListener("load",function(eventData) {
           captionator.captionify();
        },false);
</script>
```

There is a CSS subdirectory with the application, but it's there for demonstration purposes, and doesn't need to be included.

Captionator works by providing subtitles/captions using the file in whatever track element has the `default` attribute. It supports both WebVTT and SRT formatted track files. Example 3-2 shows a complete page using the *sintel_en.srt* subtitle file and Captionator to manage the subtitles.

Example 3-2. Using Captionator with a SRT subtitle file

```
<!DOCTYPE html>
<head>
   <title>Sintel with English Subtitles</title>
   <meta charset="utf-8" />
   <script src="js/captionator.js"></script>
   <script>
      window.addEventListener("load",function(eventData) {
              captionator.captionify();
           },false);
   </script>
</head>
```

```
<body>
  <video controls poster="sintelposter.jpg" width="480" height="204">
    <source src="sintel.m4v" type="video/mp4" />
    <source src="sintel.webm" type="video/webm" />
    <track label="English subtitles" kind="subtitles"
          srclang="en" src="sintel_en.srt" default />
  </video>
</body>
```

Calling the `captionify` method on the Captionator object not only turns on the subtitles, but also creates a `tracks` property on the video element. Captionator also works with WebVTT, including support for the WebVTT cues and formatting. An advantage to using the library is that it can work with your own custom controls or the default control, as shown in Figure 3-3.

Figure 3-3. Captionator in action working with Firefox's default controls

Captionator is a work in progress and not all functionality is currently available. However, it is actively supported and the future plans for the library should make it both useful and fun to use.

Playr

Figures 3-1 and 3-2, shown earlier in the chapter, were both taken while using the next tool I want to cover: Playr.

Unlike Captionator, Playr is a video player/caption/subtitle support tool, all in one. It's as simple to use as Captionator—just add the script file and a necessary CSS file to your web page, and you're ready to go. Example 3-3 contains a complete web page for playing a WebVTT formatted subtitle file with Playr.

Example 3-3. Web page incorporating use of Playr library for caption support

```
<!DOCTYPE html>
<head>
    <title>Captions</title>
    <link rel="stylesheet" href="playr.css" />
    <style>
        .grateful
        {
            background-color: orange;
            color: black;
        }
        .blood
        {
            color: red;
            font-weight: bold;
        }
    </style>
    <script src="playr.js"></script>
</head>
<body>
    <video class="playr_video">
        <source src="sintel.m4v" type="video/mp4" />
        <source src="sintel.ogv" type="video/ogg" />
        <track label="English subtitles" kind="subtitles"
                srclang="en" src="sintel.vtt" default />
    </video>
</body>
```

You will need to add a class name of ***playr_video*** to the video tag, as highlighted in the example.

When you open the page, you'll see a Menu option in the control bar. Moving your mouse over the Menu pops up a list of subtitles, captions, or other tracks that you can choose from, as shown in Figure 3-4. Playr also works with both SRT and WebVTT files. It doesn't support Flash fallback yet, but support for fallback is planned in a future release.

One thing neither Captionator nor Playr handled, at least at the time of writing, was vertical text. I found the best support for vertical text with the Leanback Player, described in the next section.

Figure 3-4. The Menu option for Playr showing the available subtitles

The Leanback Player

The Leanback Player is like Playr, in that it is a player/subtitle renderer, all in one. This program is really a set of JavaScript libraries—both for the primary functionality, and individual language-based libraries.

The Leanback Player assumes that the `video` element is structured using the Video for Everybody model, which provides not only sufficient source files for all HTML5 capable browsers, but also a fallback. You attach separate class names to the `video` element and to the fallback content.

I didn't have access to the release candidate code for the latest version of the Leanback Player, but could check out how it works with an online example at the player's web site. The primary JavaScript library and associated language libraries are loaded using script elements, as is the default CSS file:

```
<link rel="stylesheet" media="screen" href="css/leanbackPlayer_default.css"
        title="theme" />
<script type="text/javascript" src="js/leanbackPlayer.js"></script>
<script type="text/javascript" src="js/leanbackPlayer_en.js"></script>
```

The video element is included within a div element given a class attribute with a value of **leanback-player-video**. The example file shows that the track elements are defined with a different structure. I extrapolated a simplified subtext of the HTML, as follows:

```
<div class="leanback-player-video">
    <video width="532" height="300" preload="metadata" controls>
        <source src="videos/video.mp4" type="video/mp4" />
        <source src="videos/video.ogv" type="video/ogg" />
        <track enabled="true" kind="subtitles" label="Japanese" srclang="ja"
                type="text/plain" src="subtitle/japanese_ja_vertical.vtt"></track>
        <track enabled="true" kind="subtitles" label="English" srclang="en"
                type="text/plain" src="subtitle/english_en.vtt"></track>
        <track enabled="true" kind="subtitles" label="Arabic" srclang="ar"
                type="text/plain" src="subtitle/arabic_ar.vtt"></track>
    </video>
</div>
```

Notice that the track elements have start and end tags, though using the empty element syntax demonstrated in other examples should also work. But also note the use of the enabled and type attributes. These are non-standard attributes and, from looking at the JavaScript, are required for the application to work.

The Leanback Player demonstration page can be found at *http://lean backplayer.com/test/webvtt.html*. It uses another of the Blender open movie projects, Elephants Dream.

It also looks like the newer version of the code requires that the fallback content be placed into another div element, and given a class attribute with a value of **leanback-player-html-fallback**.

Nonstandard attributes aside, the newest version of the Leanback Player does an exceptional job processing the WebVTT file, including correctly handling the vertical text, as shown in Figure 3-5.

Though I focused on captions and subtitles in this section, there are other types of text tracks that are useful with HTML5 video. HTML5 media accessibility guru Silvia Pfeiffer created an excellent example of using a chapters text track for navigation at *http://www.html5videoguide .net/demos/google_io/3_navigation/*.

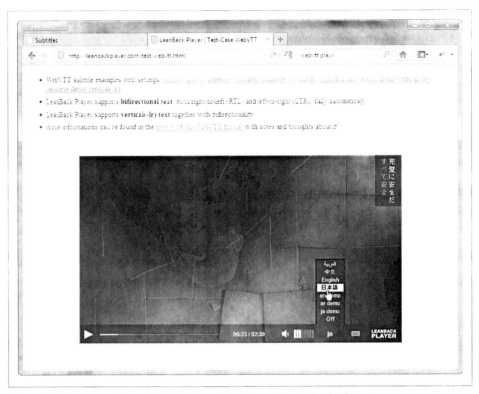

Figure 3-5. Demonstrating subtitle choice and handling of vertical subtitle text

CHAPTER 4

Advanced Media Element Scripting

The majority of HTML5 media element use focuses on their primary purpose, which is to play media resources. We might use JavaScript to craft new controls or improve the accessibility of the content, and eventually we'll see what we can do with media controllers and multiple tracks—but we'll rarely go beyond these core capabilities.

However, some folks have looked beyond the basic boxes of the video and audio element, and have demonstrated the use of these elements with other technologies, including SVG (Scalable Vector Graphics) and the canvas element. In addition, a couple of the browser companies have expanded the capability of the audio element so that it can generate sound as well as play it.

In this chapter, I'll introduce you to some of these advanced experimentation efforts with the HTML5 media elements, and provide some background so that you can give these effects a try on your own.

 Most of the material in this chapter has very limited support among browsers. The only browser capable of working with all the examples (at this time) is Firefox. I'll note browser support with each. Many of the examples are also very CPU-intensive. Use cautiously.

Media Elements and Canvas

HTML5 not only gave us the media elements, it also formalized the canvas element. The canvas element was introduced by Apple years ago, and provided a way for us to draw into an area directly in the web page. Most browsers supported the element and associated API. However, the element was standardized in HTML5 and now all of our target browsers support it.

You can combine the HTML5 media elements with canvas to create some amazing effects. Mozilla demonstrated one such effect by showing how the canvas element, combined with HTML5 video, could be used to replace the plain greenscreen background of a video with the Firefox logo. Doctor HTML5 demonstrated how to create a grayscale effect using HTML5 video and canvas. Sebastian Deutsch combined HTML5 audio with canvas and Twitter for a musical visual treat.

 Mozilla's work with canvas and HTML5 video can be found at *https://developer.mozilla.org/En/manipulating_video_using_canvas*. You can see the HTML5 Doctor's work at *http://html5doctor.com/video-canvas-magic/*. Deutsch's beautiful work can be found at *http://9elements.com/io/?p=153*. A follow-up effort that generalized the canvas/audio combination, but without Twitter, can be found at *http://nooshu.com/three-js-and-the-audio-data-api-visualisation*.

I'm going to emulate the good HTML5 Doctor's effort by creating a video filter. First, though, I'm going to go through the steps to just get the video playing in a canvas element.

Playing a Video in an Canvas Element

To play the video in a canvas, we'll need to add both the video element and the canvas element to the web page:

```
<video id="videoobj" controls width="480" height="270">
   <source src="videofile.mp4" type="video/mp4" />
   <source src="videofile.webm" type="video/webm" />
</video>
<canvas id="canvasobj" width="480" height="270"></canvas>
```

In this example, both the canvas and video elements are the same size, specified in the width and height attribute for both.

When we work with a canvas, we're really working with two different objects: the element and the *context*. The canvas element supports more than one context, but the one we're more familiar with is the two-dimensional (2D) context, created as follows:

```
var canvasObj = document.getElementById("canvasobj");
var ctx = canvasObj.getContext("2d");
```

To draw the video onto the canvas, we're going to use the 2D Canvas API method drawImage. This method takes whatever is given in the first parameter, and draws it into the canvas element. There are three versions of the drawImage method:

```
drawImage(image, dx, dy); // draw image starting at canvas position dx,dy
drawImage(image, dx, dy, dw, dh); // draw image starting at dx,dz w/dimensions dw,dh

// draw from image given image dimensions to canvas given canvas dimensions
drawImage(image, sx, sy, sw, sh, dx, dy, dw, dh);
```

The *image* shown in the methods can be one of three different types of objects:

- An `HTMLImageElement` object instance (an `img` element)
- An `HTMLCanvasElement` object instance (another `canvas` element)
- An `HTMLVideoElement` object instance (an HTML5 `video` element)

We're only interested in the last method, which takes a `video` element instance as its first parameter.

The HTMLVideoElement Interface

I haven't covered the HTMLVideoElement interface previously. In Chapter 2, I covered the HTMLMediaElement interface, but both audio and video have their own unique object interfaces: HTMLAudioElement and HTMLVideoElement, respectively.

HTMLAudioElement has little functionality beyond what HTMLMediaElement provides. HTMLVideoElement does have some additional properties:

- `height`, `width`: The height and width of the element, reflecting the `height` and `width` attributes
- `poster`: reflects the `poster` attribute
- `videoHeight`, `videoWidth`: the intrinsic height and width of the video in CSS pixels

Most of the programming functionality for the audio and video element derives from HTMLMediaElement. However, the HTMLAudioElement and HTMLVideoElement interfaces do allow us to add media appropriate functionality to each, and to restrict use to one or the other (such as restricting the first element in the `canvas` element's `drawImage` method to a video element only).

Once we have access to the `canvas` element's context and a reference to the video object, all we need to do to draw a single frame of a video object into the context (beginning at the left/top of the `canvas` element) is add the following JavaScript:

```
var videoObj = document.getElementById("videoobj");
ctx.drawImage(videoObj, 0,0);
```

The `drawImage` method isn't a *live method*, which means we have to call it every time was want to draw a video frame into the canvas. My first inclination is to use the video object's `timeupdate` event handler function to invoke the drawing action. After all, the custom control application in Chapter 2 had success using the `timeupdate` event handler to manage the playback indicator.

Incorporating the new event handler results in the application shown in Example 4-1.

Example 4-1. A first cut at drawing video data to a canvas element

```
<!DOCTYPE html>
<head>
<title>Grayscale a Video</title>
    <meta charset="utf-8" />
    <script>
        window.onload=function() {
            document.getElementById("videoobj").
                    addEventListener("timeupdate", drawVideo, false);
        }
        function drawVideo() {
            var videoObj = document.getElementById("videoobj");
            var canvasObj = document.getElementById("canvasobj");
            var ctx = canvasObj.getContext("2d");
            ctx.drawImage(videoObj,0,0);
        }
    </script>
</head>
<body>
    <video id="videoobj" controls width="480" height="270">
        <source src="videofile.mp4" type="video/mp4" />
        <source src="videofile.webm" type="video/webm" />
    </video>
    <canvas id="canvasobj" width="480" height="270"></canvas>
</body>
```

The application works in IE10, Firefox, Opera, and WebKit Nightly, but not Chrome (not even Canary), or Safari 5. However, in the browsers where the application worked, the drawing action in the canvas element was choppy, and lagged noticeably behind the video, as shown in Opera in Figure 4-1.

One of the problems with timeupdate is that it didn't fire quickly enough. Searching about through online documentation, I found that Firefox fires the timeupdate event every 250 milliseconds, and I am assuming the other browsers do something similar. Untold frames have flipped past in such a long time!

Though timeupdate was sufficient for our playback indicator, it isn't sufficient for video playback. A better approach, and one that was taken in the HTML5 Doctor article, is to use the JavaScript function setTimeout, and a time frame of 20 milliseconds—over ten times faster than using timeupdate.

The script block in Example 4-1 is modified to now use setTimeout, as shown in Example 4-2. Since we're no longer using an event that's playback-related, we also have to know when to stop drawing. The code tests to ensure that the video isn't paused or finished, first, before doing the draw.

Figure 4-1. Example 4-1 in Opera with a noticeable lag in canvas playback

Example 4-2. Updating the video/canvas application to improve performance

```
<script>
   window.onload=function() {
      document.getElementById("videoobj").
              addEventListener("play", drawVideo, false);
```

```
      }
    function drawVideo() {
      var videoObj = document.getElementById("videoobj");

      // if not playing, quit
      if (videoObj.paused || videoObj.ended) return false;

      // draw video on canvas
      var canvasObj = document.getElementById("canvasobj");
      var ctx = canvasObj.getContext("2d");
      ctx.drawImage(videoObj,0,0,480,270);
      setTimeout(drawVideo,20);
    }
  </script>
```

When we run the application with Firefox, Opera, IE10, and Webkit Nightly, we get a nice, smooth integration between the video play and the canvas drawing actions. Now we're ready to add in the filter functionality.

Creating a Video Visual Filter using the Canvas Element

To modify the presentation of the video data in the canvas element, we're actually going to need to create a new canvas element as a *scratch*, or temporary working object, place the original video data into it, apply the filter, and then access the data from the scratch canvas object and use it to update the displayed canvas object. Yes, it seems like a lot of work, but it's necessary. We can modify canvas data, but we can't directly modify video data. And we don't want to use our display canvas element to perform all our manipulation.

 Security protocols currently prohibit accessing the canvas data if the image used (regardless of whether it's video or a still image) is accessed from a domain other than the one serving the web page with the canvas application.

The filter function we're using is one that's also been used with still images and the canvas element. It's basically a desaturation of the color to create a grayscale effect. I modified a filter for still images I found at the HTML5 Rocks web site. It's very similar to the same filter used in the HTML5 Doctor article:

```
        function grayScale(pixels) {
           var d = pixels.data;
           for (var i=0; i<d.length; i+=4) {
              var r = d[i];
              var g = d[i+1];
              var b = d[i+2];
              var v = 0.2126*r + 0.7152*g + 0.0722*b;
              d[i] = d[i+1] = d[i+2] = v
           }
          return pixels;
        }
```

The canvas pixel data is sent to the filter, which does the grayscale conversion and then returns the data. Example 4-3 shows the script block incorporating the new filter.

Example 4-3. Using a scratch canvas to create a grayscale of the video

```
<script>

  // grayscale filter
  function grayScale(pixels) {
    var d = pixels.data;
    for (var i=0; i<d.length; i+=4) {
      var r = d[i];
      var g = d[i+1];
      var b = d[i+2];
      var v = 0.2126*r + 0.7152*g + 0.0722*b;
      d[i] = d[i+1] = d[i+2] = v
    }
    return pixels;
  }

  // event listeners
  window.onload=function() {
    document.getElementById("videoobj").
            addEventListener("play", drawVideo, false);
  }

  // draw the video
  function drawVideo() {
    var videoObj = document.getElementById("videoobj");

    // if not playing, quit
    if (videoObj.paused || videoObj.ended) return false;

    // create scratch canvas
    var canvasObj = document.getElementById("canvasobj");
    var bc = document.createElement("canvas");
    bc.width=480;
    bc.height=270;

    // get contexts for scratch and display canvases
    var ctx = canvasObj.getContext("2d");
    var ctx2 = bc.getContext("2d");

    // draw video on scratch and get its data
    ctx2.drawImage(videoObj, 0, 0, 480, 270);
    var pData = ctx2.getImageData(0,0,480,270);

    // grayscale it and set to display canvas
    pData = grayScale(pData);
    ctx.putImageData(pData,0,0);

    setTimeout(drawVideo,20);
  }
</script>
```

Figure 4-2 shows the grayscale filter in action in Webkit Nightly. The grayscale effect also works with IE10, Firefox, and Opera.

Figure 4-2. Video and video in grayscale using canvas

The HTML5 Rocks site had some other interesting filters to apply against the video element (if you have the CPU for the task). One in particular, though, struck me as quite useful and a good justification for the use of such a filter: being able to increase or decrease the brightness of the video.

I created a global variable, brightness, used to track the current video's brightness setting. I also added two new buttons to the web page: one to decrease the brightness level of the video, and one to increase it.

Next, I added a new filter function, adjBrightness, that takes pixel data and an adjustment indicator to increase or decrease the brightness of the video:

```
function adjBrightness(pixels, adjustment) {
    var d = pixels.data;
    for (var i=0; i<d.length; i+=4) {
        d[i] += adjustment;
        d[i+1] += adjustment;
        d[i+2] += adjustment;
    }
    return pixels;
}
```

I also added event listeners to the button elements' click events. In the click event handler functions, the code increases or decreases the brightness variable accordingly. Example 4-4 contains the complete web page.

Example 4-4. Video playback in canvas with brightness controls

```
<!DOCTYPE html>
<head>
<title>Adjust Video Brightness</title>
    <meta charset="utf-8" />
    <style>
        #backcanvas { display: none; }
    </style>
    <script>

        var brightness = 0;

        // adjust brightness
        function adjBrightness(pixels, adjustment) {
            var d = pixels.data;
            for (var i=0; i<d.length; i+=4) {
                d[i] += adjustment;
                d[i+1] += adjustment;
                d[i+2] += adjustment;
            }
            return pixels;
        }
        window.onload=function() {
            document.getElementById("videoobj").
                    addEventListener("play", drawVideo, false);

            // brighten video
            document.getElementById("increase").
                    addEventListener("click",function() {
                        brightness+=5;
                        },false);
```

```
    // darken video
    document.getElementById("decrease").
            addEventListener("click",function() {
                brightness-=5;
                },false);
        }
    function drawVideo() {
        var videoObj = document.getElementById("videoobj");

        // if not playing, quit
        if (videoObj.paused || videoObj.ended) return false;

        // access draw canvas, create scratch canvas
        var canvasObj = document.getElementById("canvasobj");
        var bc = document.createElement("canvas");
        bc.width=480;
        bc.height=270;

        // get context for both canvas objects
        var ctx = canvasObj.getContext("2d");
        var ctx2 = bc.getContext("2d");

        // draw video on scratch canvas obj, get data
        ctx2.drawImage(videoObj, 0, 0);
        var pData = ctx2.getImageData(0,0,480,270);

        // adjust brightness and set to display canvas
        pData = adjBrightness(pData, brightness);
        ctx.putImageData(pData,0,0);

        setTimeout(drawVideo,20);
    }

    </script>
</head>
<body>
    <video id="videoobj" controls width="480" height="270">
        <source src="videofile.mp4" type="video/mp4" />
        <source src="videofile.webm" type="video/webm" />
    </video>
    <canvas id="canvasobj" width="480" height="270"></canvas>
<div>
<button id="increase">Increase brightness</button>
<button id="decrease">Decrease brightness</button>
</body>
```

The use of the brightness filter works with Firefox, Webkit Nightly, and IE10. You can adjust the filter in Opera but you get truly bizarre results if you do.

To incorporate this functionality as part of your custom control, hide the video and display the **canvas** element, instead. Figure 4-3 shows the brightness filter in action. The top picture is from the video, and the bottom picture is the brightness-adjusted canvas. I actually think the brightness-adjusted canvas is an improvement. Also notice in the image a slight lag in the video playback, even with our improved event handling.

Figure 4-3. Demonstrating the new brightness control implemented using the canvas element

Access the different canvas image filters at HTML5 Rocks at *http://www .html5rocks.com/en/tutorials/canvas/imagefilters/*.

WebGL, Video, and Security Concerns

You might be asking yourself whether there's a 3D context for the canvas element. Well, there is: WebGL.

WebGL is an open source effort managed by the non-profit Khronos Group. It's based on the OpenGL ES 2.0 specification, and has support in Chrome, Firefox, and development releases of Safari and Opera.

WebGL is capable of integrating video into its three-dimensional effects. However, recent security concerns about WebGL has led to recommendations from Context Information Security LTD and the United States Computer Emergency Readiness Team (US-CERT) to not use WebGL and that people disable WebGL support in their browsers.

One of the security issues was directly related to the ability to use a canvas element that contains content (image or video) from a domain other than the domain hosting the application, as a WebGL texture. As a workaround, a new attribute (crossorigin) was added to the video and audio elements, as well as the img element. This attribute basically enables (or disables) the use of a cross-domain image or video file in WebGL textures, unless the appropriate communication between the browser and the remote web server occurs, through the concept of Cross-Origin Resource Sharing (or CORS for short).

The crossorigin attribute does not fix the problem that originated the security concern, but sandboxes it as a way of hopefully limiting the damage that could be generated by a security breach. It's a very recent addition to the HTML5 specification that's currently being debated, and may not survive to the final recommended version of HTML5.

You can find more on WebGL security concerns related to the canvas element (and HTML video) at *http://www.contextis.com/resources/blog/webgl/*, and more on WebGL at *http://www.khronos.org/*.

Media Elements and SVG

In March 2010, Paul Irish wrote about spending some time with folks proficient with SVG, and provided a web page demonstrating how to use SVG and HTML5. At Webjam8, Andreas Bovens demonstrated the use of HTML5 media elements with SVG and SMIL. Mike Thomas showed how to use SVG masks with video to beautiful effect. Mr. Doob demonstrated how to combine SVG and HTML5 audio to create a 3D Waveform. Erik Dahlström created a terrific music video based, in part, on the use of SVG patterns.

Combining HTML5 media elements and SVG is combining the best of the old and new from the W3C. The HTML5 media elements are new, but already demonstrate robustness and extensibility. SVG has been around for over a decade and with the advent of HTML5, is now supported in HTML as well as XHTML.

There are two ways you can combine the HTML5 media elements with SVG: using the SVG capabilities with media elements within an HTML document, or embedding an HTML5 media element within an SVG document.

Mike Thomas's demonstration combining HTML5 video with SVG masks can be found at *http://atomicrobotdesign.com/blog/htmlcss/svg -masks-html5-video-and-firefox-4/*. Andreas Bovens' presentation can be seen at *http://my.opera.com/ODIN/blog/2008/10/20/my-webjam-8 -presentation-on-builder-au-cool-things-with-html5-svg-and-smil*, though the examples no longer work. Paul Irish's demo page and video can be found at *http://paulirish.com/2010/svg-filters-on-html5-video/*. Mr. Doob's Waveform can be launched at *http://www.chromeexperi ments.com/detail/3d-waveform/*. Erik Dahlström's work can be seen at the SVGWow page, *http://svg-wow.org/blog/2011/03/28/rotozoom -video/*.

Adding an HTML5 Video to an SVG Document

Most demonstrations of using SVG and HTML5 video together are based on SVG and the video element embedded into an HTML or XHTML document. However, Chris Double created a nice video/SVG demonstration page where multiple videos are stacked in a web page, and can be resized and rotated about using SVG functionality.

The real issue with using videos in SVG is that SVG is famous for being able to scale without degrading. Video, on the other hand, does not scale. If you increase the size of the video file, all you'll get is a blurry, pixelated picture.

Still, if you're familiar with SVG, it's fun to give HTML5 video and SVG a try.

Find out about Chris Double's efforts with HTML5 video and SVG at *http://www.bluishcoder.co.nz/2007/08/svg-video-demo.html*. Access the video/SVG demo at *http://double.co.nz/video_test/video.svg*. Note that the demo only works in Firefox and Opera.

An SVG document is XML, which means we have to make sure our attribute values are quoted, our tags are closed, and values assigned to boolean attributes. HTML within SVG documents is added using a specialized element, foreignObject. When you add an HTML block to an SVG document, you're telling the user agent not to process the contents as SVG, but as HTML. Typically the block is added as a body element, complete with HTML namespace.

Why would you include video within an SVG document? One reason is to make use of the more sophisticated graphics available with SVG. For instance, you could provide a more interesting frame for the video element. Example 4-5 shows an SVG document with an embedded video, nested within a rectangle with a pink background and a green dashed border.

Example 4-5. HTML5 video embedded in an SVG document

```
<?xml version="1.0"?>
<svg xmlns="http://www.w3.org/2000/svg"
width="510px" height="300px" viewBox="0 0 510 300">

<rect x="10" y="10" width="490" height="280"
      stroke="green" stroke-width="10"  stroke-linejoin="round"
      stroke-dasharray="5,3,2" fill="pink" />

<g id="videoobj">
  <foreignObject viewBox="0 0 480 270" width="480px"
     height="270px" x="15" y="15">
     <body xmlns="http://www.w3.org/1999/xhtml"
          style="margin: 0; padding: 0">
        <video controls="controls" width="480" height="270">
           <source src="videofile.mp4" type="video/mp4" />
           <source src="videofile.ogg" type="video/ogg" />
        </video>
     </body>
  </foreignObject>
</g>
</svg>
```

Notice in the code how I had to assign a value to the controls boolean attribute. If I didn't, I'd get the dreaded orange screen of death for Firefox that appears when you send bad XML to the browser.

Figure 4-4 shows my masterpiece in Webkit Nightly. The application also works in Firefox, Chrome, Safari, but not in IE9/IE10 or Opera.

Well, OK, the visual impact of my work of art is nothing to write home about. But another advantage to SVG is being able to find openly available SVG documents throughout the Web, and being able to modify these documents for your own use. Figure 4-5 shows a slightly better graphic to use for the HTML video element.

Figure 4-4. HTML5 video playing, framed by SVG

Figure 4-5. HTML5 video playing within a TV frame in a found SVG file

The advantage of SVG is that all of the graphics are individually accessible markup elements. Having the primitives makes it simple to find what you need and modify it to match the result you want. Best of all, the graphics can be easily scaled to whatever dimensions you need.

 I found the TV SVG graphic at *http://www.openclipart.org/*, the best place to find public domain SVG you can use in your projects.

Embedding HTML in SVG can be fun, if a little challenging. Most uses of SVG with HTML5 video, though, are to borrow many of the SVG capabilities for use with an HTML5 video within an HTML5 document, as discussed next.

 If you have the same size image and video, you could also just use an absolutely positioned PNG element and get much the same effect, as demonstrated by Chris Mills at *http://people.opera.com/cmills/video _mask/*.

Applying SVG Filters to Video Files within HTML

An interesting use of SVG and HTML5 video together is to apply SVG filters or masks or other graphical devices to the video element.

SVG filters are highly sophisticated effects that can be used individually or combined into more complex presentations. These filters are declarative effects that can be applied to SVG elements, but can also be applied to any HTML, including HTML media elements.

To use an SVG filter with an HTML5 video element within an HTML5 document, we'll have to add an SVG block to the same HTML file that has the video:

```
<!DOCTYPE html>
<head>
    <title>SVG filter effects with video</title>
    <meta charset="utf-8" />
</head>
<body>
    <video controls poster="poster.jpg">
        <source src="videofile.mp4" type="video/mp4" />
        <source src="videofile.webm" type="video/webm" />
    </video>
    <svg id='image' version="1.1">
    </svg>

</body>
```

Filters are created within a defs (definitions) element, and given unique identifiers. To apply the filter to the video, the filter identifier is used within a CSS style setting:

```
<style>
  video { filter:url(#filtername); }
</style>
```

The CSS filter property takes one value, the url function, passing in the filter's identifier.

To demonstrate, we'll create one of the simpler filter effects: a filter that takes a color video and converts it to black and white. This particular effect is created using the feColorMatric filter, which applies a matrix transformation on the RGBA color and alpha values of each pixel in the original element, in this case a video. The matrix structure is as follows:

```
| R' |     | a00 a01 a02 a03 a04 |     | R |
| G' |     | a10 a11 a12 a13 a14 |     | G |
| B' |  =  | a20 a21 a22 a23 a24 |  *  | B |
| A' |     | a30 a31 a32 a33 a34 |     | A |
| 1  |     | 0   0   0   0   1   |     | 1 |
```

The actual value passed to the grayscale filter effect is:

```
0.3333 0.3333 0.3333 0 0
0.3333 0.3333 0.3333 0 0
0.3333 0.3333 0.3333 0 0
0      0      0      1 0
```

Example 4-6 has a complete page with HTML video and applied SVG filter. Pay particular attention to the fact that no JavaScript is used to create the effect.

Example 4-6. Applying an SVG filter to an HTML5 video within an HTML document

```
<!DOCTYPE html>
<head>
<title>Video</title>
  <meta charset="utf-8" />
  <style>
    video { filter:url(#blackandwhite); border: 2px solid red;}
  </style>
</head>
<body>
  <video controls poster="poster.jpg" autoplay>
    <source src="videofile.mp4" type="video/mp4" />
    <source src="videofile.webm" type="video/webm" />
  </video>
  <svg id='image' version="1.1">
    <defs>
      <filter id="blackandwhite">
        <feColorMatrix values="0.3333 0.3333 0.3333 0 0
                    0.3333 0.3333 0.3333 0 0
                    0.3333 0.3333 0.3333 0 0
                    0      0      0      1 0"/>
```

```
        </filter>
      </defs>
    </svg>
  </body>
```

Figure 4-6 shows the video playing in Firefox...the only browser that supports the effect.

Figure 4-6. Applying an SVG filter to an HTML5 video

Mozilla created the concept of applying SVG filters (and masks and other graphical devices) to HTML elements within an HTML document. No other browser has taken up the idea, though I hope they eventually do so. As you can see, the code is quite simple, and doesn't require any JavaScript.

As much as I like this ability, though, there are performance issues with applying SVG effects against HTML elements in this manner. I created an offscreen illumination effect for one example, and thought my laptop's fan would fly out of the case—and my laptop is usually sufficient to meet the needs of even the most tortuously complex web page effect.

 For more on applying SVG filters to HTML documents, see the support page for the effect at Mozilla, at *https://developer.mozilla.org/En/Apply ing_SVG_effects_to_HTML_content.*

The Audio Data APIs

It's easy to focus on the HTML5 `video` element and forget that the specification also includes a wonderful new facility to add audio to the web page. The `audio` element is just as easy to work with as the `video` element, and the HTMLMediaElement and other API functionality works equally well with the `audio` element.

What isn't part of the HTML5 or any other specification is functionality that is only relevant to the audio type: the Audio Data APIs. The Audio Data APIs are a set of APIs being worked on by Mozilla, Google, and Webkit—though not all on the same API—to add an API that not only provides audio playback, but also audio generation, too.

Matt Hobbs had fun with the Audio Data API. He extrapolated Mr. Doob's efforts discussed earlier in the chapter and combined the canvas visual effects with the Audio Data API. Greg Jopa combined Mozilla's Audio Data API with the VexFlow music notation rendering API to create an extraordinary web page-based online musical instrument.

> Matt Hobb's work combining canvas and the Audio Data API can be seen at *http://nooshu.com/three-js-and-the-audio-data-api-visualisation*. The work by Greg Jopa combining the Audio Data API and VexFlow can be explored at *http://www.gregjopa.com/2010/12/html5-guitar-tab-player-with-firefox-audio-data-api/*.

The Mozilla Audio Data API provides a way to get an array of values representing the audio sample data. Though related to audio, evidently the functionality can be applied to the `audio` and `video` element, though you'll have access only to the audio data.

To access the data, add an event listener for the `MozDataAvailable` event to the media element. In the event handler function, the event object provides access to the audio data through the `frameBuffer.` Mozilla provides an example that actually takes this data and prints it out to the page. I copied portions of it in Example 4-7.

Example 4-7. Printing out the audio data to the web page

```
<!DOCTYPE html>
<html>
  <head>
    <title>JavaScript Visualization Example</title>
    <body>
    <audio id="audio-element"
          src="sharecropper.ogg"
          controls>
    </audio>
        <pre id="raw">hello</pre>
    <script>
      function audioAvailable(event) {
        var frameBuffer = event.frameBuffer;
        var t = event.time;
```

```
        var text = "Samples at: " + t + "\n";
        text += frameBuffer[0] + "   " + frameBuffer[1]
        raw.innerHTML = text;
      }

      var raw = document.getElementById('raw')
      var audio = document.getElementById('audio-element');
      audio.addEventListener('MozAudioAvailable', audioAvailable, false);

    </script>
  </body>
</html>
```

It's important to understand that audio can be represented textually, because the Audio Data API can be used to actually generate sound, as well as play sound. Another example that Mozilla provides, shown in Example 4-8, produces a tone—though in fact, a rather annoying tone.

Example 4-8. Generating a tone using the Audio Data API

```
<!doctype html>
<html>
  <head>
    <title>Generating audio in real time</title>
    <script type="text/javascript">
    function playTone() {
      var output = new Audio();
     output.mozSetup(1, 44100);
      var samples = new Float32Array(22050);
      var len = samples.length;

      for (var i = 0; i < samples.length ; i++) {
        samples[i] = Math.sin( i / 20 );
      }
            output.mozWriteAudio(samples);
    }
  </script>
  </head>
  <body>
    <p>This demo plays a one second tone when you click the button below.</p>
    <button onclick="playTone();">Play</button>
  </body>
</html>
```

Though the result is simple, consider the capability this API provides: the ability to not only play audio files without having to use a plug-in, but also to generate audio. Game developers in particular should be interested in this capability.

As I mentioned earlier, there is no specification work underway for the Audio Data API, most likely because the work on the concept is still very new. Apple and Google are also exploring an audio data API via work in WebKit, called the Web Audio API. Google did propose the formation of a W3C Audio Group, but none has been created at this time.

Do check out the APIs and the many excellent examples, but remain cautious about using the APIs in your production efforts.

The Audio Data API MozillaWiki entry can be found at *https://wiki.mo zilla.org/Audio_Data_API*. Mozilla has also provided an introduction to the API at *https://developer.mozilla.org/en/Introducing_the_Audio_API _Extension*. The BBC has also provided an excellent tutorial/introduction to the Audio Data API at *http://www.bbc.co.uk/blogs/researchand development/2010/11/mozilla-audio-data-api.shtml*. Access more information on the Web Audio API at *http://chromium.googlecode.com/svn/ trunk/samples/audio/index.html*.

HTML Media Frameworks and Tools

It's actually quite a bit of fun coding a media controller. However, sometimes we don't have the time or the inclination (or enough familiarity with JavaScript) to create our own media custom controls and other applications. That's when we look to see what others have already created that we can use.

As new as HTML5 media elements are, there are already several different useful libraries, plug-ins, and applications for working with HTML5 media elements. This appendix briefly outlines some of the more interesting I've found.

Subtitle/Caption Rendering Library

The only library I tested that manages subtitles and captions and that isn't also a video player is Captionator. I covered Captionator in Chapter 3, and you can download the code and find out more about the project at *https://github.com/cgiffard/Captionator*.

Video Players

There's a wealth of video players you can download, ready to use. Some are created as plug-ins that you can pop into your environment. Others are libraries you need to install and set up for use in your pages. Some provide custom controls to play the video, while others also render subtitle or caption files associated with the video.

In Chapter 2, I covered two video players that also render subtitle files: Playr and the Leanback Player. Both players work with SRT, as well as WebVTT files. You can download Playr at *http://www.delphiki.com/html5/playr/*, and Leanback Player at *http://dev.mennerich.name/showroom/html5_video/*. The Leanback Player also has WordPress and Joomla plug-ins.

VideoJS is a sophisticated and polished player that can be used as a standalone player—or as a WordPress, Drupal, or jQuery Plug-in; an Umbraco Utility; or a Joomla Extension. It's 100% skinnable using CSS, and includes predefined skins that enable the player to emulate well-known video environments, such as YouTube. It, like most of the players, also provides fullscreen video support. Not to leave any HTML5 video stone uncovered, VideoJS also supports subtitles (SRT only). You can access the primary VideoJS web site at *http://videojs.com/*.

Another subtitle-supporting video player is jMediaElement, a solid video player that also has excellent keyboard support. You can access the player at *http://www.protofunc .com/jme/*. Unlike most other subtitle-rendering players, though, jMediaElement doesn't support the track element, and only supports SRT files.

The Kaltura HTML5 Media Library provides a clean, cross-browser-friendly interface to the HTML5 video element. It's also skinnable, and has been built to be easily extended. Kaltura is built in jQuery and the jQuery UI. Both the Wikimedia Foundation and the Internet Archive have chosen the Kaltura HTML5 Video Player for playing videos in their own pages. Read more about and download the Kaltura HTML5 Media library at *http://html5video.org/*.

Projekktor is an HTML5 video player that allows you to add images and ads to the video during playback. It also provides a way to incorporate an audio player and one cover image, as well as creating and working with playlists (rather than just a single audio or video file). Discover more about Projekktor at *http://www.projekktor.com/*.

 If you don't like the video players I've featured, check out a page featuring 19 different HTML5 video players, put together by Philip Bräunlich, at *http://praegnanz.de/html5video/index.php*.

Audio Only or Audio/Video Players

Not wanting to leave audio out of the fun, jPlayer is a jQuery-based audio and video player with an extremely clean, Apple-like interface. You can find out more about the player at *http://www.jplayer.org/*.

The Zen audio player is a fork of jPlayer solely for playing audio. It provides a very clean interface, as well as a nice visual effect while the audio resource is playing. You can read more about and try Zen Player at *http://lab.simurai.com/ui/zen-player/*.

Another library providing a clean cross-browser interface for the HTML5 audio element is audio.js, available at *http://kolber.github.com/audiojs/*.

Speakker provides an impressive radio-like display for audio files. It's built on top of jQuery (something many HTML5 libraries have in common). You don't embed an audio element into the web page, but instantiate the Speakker control into another HTML element, (most likely a div element). And you don't point the application at single audio files, but to a PHP page that provides a JSON-based playlist. The application makes use of Projekktor, discussed in the prior section.

Check out a demo or download the software, following the detailed installation instructions at *http://www.speakker.com/*.

Other Libraries, Utilities, and Toys

I covered a couple of video and audio encoding tools in Chapter 1, but didn't cover one that actually works in your Firefox browser: Fireogg. Fireogg is a Firefox extension that can take your H.264 video and create a Ogg video. Not only does it encode, but you can tweak the size and quality of the resulting encoded video. Access FireOgg with your Firefox browser at *http://firefogg.org/*.

When Google made its announcement that it would no longer support H.264 (MP4) videos, Microsoft created an extension to enable Chrome to play H.264 videos. You can access the extension at *http://www.interoperabilitybridges.com/wmp-extension-for-chrome*.

The riffwave.js library is an interesting little beastie. It encodes audio data into a format (PCM inside a RIFF container) that can be played in an HTML5 audio element. It doesn't generate a sound file, but a data URI that you then pass to a new HTML5 audio element:

```
var wave = new RIFFWAVE(data); // create the wave file
var audio = new Audio(wave.dataURI); // create the HTML5 audio element
audio.play();
```

A data URI is a encoded text string that allows us to include image or other data inline. Download the riffwave.js library at *http://www.codebase.es/riffwave/*.

Patternsketch is an online audio sequencer and drum machine that you can use to create audio patterns that you can then download as a WAV, OGG, or MP3 file. Create your audio pattern using Patternsketch at *http://patternsketch.com/*.

You can also upload your Patternsketch audio file to Sound Cloud, an online cloud service that allows you to create, store, and share your sound files. Sound Cloud can be accessed at *http://soundcloud.com*.

Moving from the HTML5 media elements—specifically, to HTML5 in general—the Modernizer library is a way of ensuring that your HTML5 applications work equally well in all browsers (or, at a minimum, degrades without major breakage). You can find Modernizer at *http://modernizr.com/*.

If you want to know which browsers support what HTML5 features, the HTML5 Test site lets you know how your browser compares, at *http://html5test.com/*. You can also find out when you can use one HTML5 feature or another at When Can I Use... (at *http://caniuse.com/*).

About the Author

Shelley Powers has been working with and writing about web technologies—from the first release of JavaScript to the latest graphics and design tools—for more than 15 years. Her recent O'Reilly books have covered the semantic web, Ajax, JavaScript, and web graphics. She's an avid amateur photographer and web development aficionado.

Get even more for your money.

Join the O'Reilly Community, and register the O'Reilly books you own. It's free, and you'll get:

- $4.99 ebook upgrade offer
- 40% upgrade offer on O'Reilly print books
- Membership discounts on books and events
- Free lifetime updates to ebooks and videos
- Multiple ebook formats, DRM FREE
- Participation in the O'Reilly community
- Newsletters
- Account management
- 100% Satisfaction Guarantee

Signing up is easy:

1. **Go to: oreilly.com/go/register**
2. **Create an O'Reilly login.**
3. **Provide your address.**
4. **Register your books.**

Note: English-language books only

To order books online:
oreilly.com/store

For questions about products or an order:
orders@oreilly.com

To sign up to get topic-specific email announcements and/or news about upcoming books, conferences, special offers, and new technologies:
elists@oreilly.com

For technical questions about book content:
booktech@oreilly.com

To submit new book proposals to our editors:
proposals@oreilly.com

O'Reilly books are available in multiple DRM-free ebook formats. For more information:
oreilly.com/ebooks

Spreading the knowledge of innovators   oreilly.com

©2010 O'Reilly Media, Inc. O'Reilly logo is a registered trademark of O'Reilly Media, Inc. 00000

The information you need, when and where you need it.

With Safari Books Online, you can:

Access the contents of thousands of technology and business books

- Quickly search over 7000 books and certification guides
- Download whole books or chapters in PDF format, at no extra cost, to print or read on the go
- Copy and paste code
- Save up to 35% on O'Reilly print books
- **New!** Access mobile-friendly books directly from cell phones and mobile devices

Stay up-to-date on emerging topics before the books are published

- Get on-demand access to evolving manuscripts.
- Interact directly with authors of upcoming books

Explore thousands of hours of video on technology and design topics

- Learn from expert video tutorials
- Watch and replay recorded conference sessions

Spreading the knowledge of innovators   safari.oreilly.com

©2009 O'Reilly Media, Inc. O'Reilly logo is a registered trademark of O'Reilly Media, Inc. 00000

CPSIA information can be obtained at www.ICGtesting.com
Printed in the USA
LVOW111515140213

320146LV00006B/347/P

9 781449 304454